WHEN HEAVEN CALLS

WHEN HEAVEN CALLS

Life Lessons from America's Top Psychic Medium

Matt Fraser

G

GALLERY BOOKS

New York   London   Toronto   Sydney   New Delhi

· CONTENTS ·

This book is dedicated to my family, fans,
and loved ones in spirit. I couldn't pick just one person
because I love you all so much.
All of you played a role in helping to get me
where I am today.
So here goes . . .

✝ *Grandma Mary:* Thank you for the many visits from the spirit world and for always guiding me and leading me to my spiritual path.

✝ *Poppy:* Thank you for coming with me to so many of my shows and being so supportive. I will never forget our car rides together and how proud you were to see me do what I love.

Mom: Thank you for loving me and helping me find my own psychic voice. It was with your love and encouragement that I found my strength on the world stage.

Dad: Thank you for putting your own beliefs aside so that you could love and support me with who I am. It is because of you that I can face even the toughest skeptics.

Maria: Thank you for being my best friend and being here right alongside me during this crazy ride. Thank you for putting so much on hold so that you could help me achieve my psychic dream.

My Fans and Followers: Thank you for trusting me with delivering messages from your loved ones in spirit. It is because of you that I am where I am today. Thank you for recommending me and being so loyal. I will not let you down.

Team Fraser: Thank you to everyone on my spiritual team. I want to thank my CFO, publicist, LA marketing team, drivers, and PAs who allow me to do what I do best. You know who you are.

The Skeptics: Thank you for testing and challenging me. It was because of you that I realized I had to look deeper into my ability and work hard. You made me realize that now it's more important than ever that my messages are heard.

Sharon and Anthony and Theo and Ava: Thank you for accepting me into your family and also for supporting me. It's not every day that your daughter/sister is in a relationship with a psychic medium. Having your blessing is a beautiful feeling.

Last But Never Least—Alexa: I cannot thank you enough for being right here by my side. Thank you for traveling with me across the country, waiting for me at home after a show, and all the little things you do like having a coffee ready for me to wake up to the morning of a big show. Thank you for the endless love and kindness that you show me every day. Thank you for being my rock when life gets overwhelming, and reminding me how special I am.

A Message from Matt's Longtime Publicist

One day my life was changed forever. I received an email from a young psychic medium named Matt Fraser. He had heard good things about me and thought I would do great PR campaigns for him and put him in the news so he could help more people.

When we spoke, he explained that he was currently an EMT working in security at the Boston Seaport Hotel and World Trade Center. Matt had my total undivided attention as he spontaneously gave me messages from my deceased dad, Murray. Apparently, my dad knew the exact challenges I was experiencing in my marriage and with both of my sons. I hadn't shared any of this online. In fact, I had kept it all hidden, trying to deal with it in secret.

Talking with Matt was five minutes of total surprise. First I was crying, then laughing. My dad has a sense of humor even in heaven! That was it; I was all in.

Matt later explained that his deceased grandmother Mary, who was also a psychic medium, suggested he contact me. I owe his grandma Mary a huge thank-you!

Everything about Matt is extraordinary: his gift of psychic medium abilities to do readings, to see visions like in a movie, to hear messages with names and specific details, to feel the illnesses that a departed loved one died from, to offer the listener comfort, and show them that love is eternal. His abilities continue to astound me. He has the highest integrity, and I am so very honored to have received the call that lifted up my spirit and has allowed me to help him reach millions.

Although you may see Matt on TV shows or listen to him give radio readings to total strangers who call in with only a first name, or read an article in a magazine or see a video online, it is only part of what he does. Behind the scenes, camera crews and producers frequently get readings when Matt walks by them and a loved one in heaven appears before him, asking to share information that will ease a family member's sorrow or confusion.

On radio shows, staff members line the hallways asking Matt for messages. He has even worked with several detectives to help solve crimes. He often does charity events to help the causes dear to his heart. Despite it all, Matt enjoys life and is a deeply devoted family man who has a highly developed sense of humor and is constantly seeing the positive in life.

I think you will find Matt's book to be surprising and highly entertaining. This is his true life story, and I hope you are comforted by the touching moments and energized by the compassion and humor detailed within these pages. As Matt always says, "Love is eternal and everlasting."

Best,

Imal Wagner

WHEN
HEAVEN
CALLS

CHAPTER 1

Heaven Calls!

HANG ON, SPIRIT; I HAVEN'T HAD MY COFFEE YET!

People not in the habit of chatting with the dead have a hard time imagining what my life must be like. Based on some of the comments and questions I receive, I'm pretty sure they think I spend most of my day sitting cross-legged in a trance, maybe hovering a few inches off the ground, leaving Rhode Island and my physical body behind as I journey across the veil to the spirit realm, before making a quick stop at a psychic tearoom to read coffee grounds and gaze into a crystal ball.

It's really not like that at all. The real Matt Fraser is just an ordinary guy who just so happens to speak to dead people. I am an open book and I am happy to share a typical day in a not-so-ordinary life.

It's eight a.m., and the alarm buzzes. I'm not a morning person so I start the day hitting snooze seven or eight times. Staying in bed isn't an option with three or four public events per week, private readings every afternoon, and frequent appearances on TV and radio shows. Sometimes my schedule is so hectic I forget what day of the week it is or what city I will even be visiting. I try to motivate myself by starting the day with a song. I love all kinds of music, but nothing gets me going like old disco and pop; yeah, I guess you can say I am an old soul. I've programmed a special mix just for mornings. Today it's "Manic Monday" by The Bangles, followed by Gloria Gaynor belting out "I Will Survive." Okay, Gloria, I'm awake now!

I might listen to other stuff during the day, but swear by my upbeat morning mix. I can't afford to let my energy lag because my line of work involves creating an inviting space for spirits. Just like the rest of us, spirits prefer to spend time where the energy is upbeat and they feel good. And it's not just the spirits. Clients feel my energy too. They feel better if I'm open, alert, and positive.

I check my phone calendar—it's going to be another busy day. And it looks like my morning playlist was successful in raising my energy because I start receiving messages from the other side as soon as I step in the shower. A little flash—a vision, if you will— gets my attention and helps me to actually see the person whose soul is reaching out to me. Then the image fades and I can now feel them, hear their thoughts, and often get an impression of how they died. After that, little messages start to follow. Luckily, I don't fully experience what they felt when they died, but I do get a tingling sensation or heaviness in the area of my body that parallels the affected area of theirs.

This morning's visitor in spirit is a young man in his early twenties. As I am in the shower getting ready for the day, I start to see visions of him; he looks pale and thin. A tingling sensation around my heart and a fuzzy feeling in my head makes me pretty sure this poor guy overdosed. I know this reading is going to be an emotional one, but first I need to make a quick stop.

PSYCHICS RUN ON DUNKIN'

I get dressed and jump in my car to make a coffee run. I think about the visions that came through in the shower—likely a preview of what's to come in one of my afternoon Skype readings. This guy is obviously eager and likely to be the first one through the door for that reading, so to speak, but once he's had his say, other souls will also show up. He's still nudging me, trying to get his message through. If I don't tune in 100 percent, they keep pushing until I listen, getting louder and louder until they have my full attention. Mom says it's like having a toddler around when you're trying to talk on the phone.

Hang on, I tell his spirit. *Coffee first!*

I maneuver my car through the Dunkin' drive-through and shout my large regular iced hazelnut order. I used to get a small, but the new peel-and-reveal promo is irresistible, not to mention I won't have time later for a refill!

A disembodied voice crackles through the little speaker.

"Is this Matt Fraser?"

Sorry to disappoint, but this is no ghost. Sharon at the take-out window knows my voice after her grandmother came through loud and clear last week. Grandma had some doubts about the new young man in her granddaughter's life and wouldn't rest until I assured her Sharon was fine. Sometimes the soul can't be denied. Messages must be delivered even in the drive-through and despite the fellow coffee addicts honking anxiously behind me. The message made her entire day. She was so happy I even got a free donut that day!

Here in Rhode Island—a state you can drive through in forty-five minutes without traffic—I'm often recognized. Frequent TV appearances and live events help ensure that I'm always running into people who tell me how much I've helped them or someone close to them. It doesn't bother me. I find it to be the biggest reward, and I am so thankful to have this gift to share.

I head home with coffee and a glazed donut—a pretty ordinary beginning to the workday.

THIS OFFICE IS GETTING CROWDED!

Sitting at my desk, I field routine calls—planning upcoming events, a celebrity cruise, T-shirt orders, et cetera. I also spend an hour or so each day catching up with my fans. I love signing into my Facebook and social media accounts and seeing so many comments and notifications. I try my hardest to reply to as many as I possibly can because I feel part of my role as a medium isn't just speaking to the dead, but also inspiring the living with the divine knowledge heaven has taught me. After replying to comments, I create inspirational, uplifting quotes and pictures to share with my followers. I am always so humbled by the thousands of people who read these from all over the world. My social media channels become so much more than fan pages. They have become an online community where it is safe to share your experiences and learn the language of spirit. It's all part of my mission to help the living heal from grief.

Where would I be without my to-do list? I have to be extra focused because I don't just get normal interruptions like ringing doorbells, cats demanding a scratch behind the ears, or calls from girlfriends. Spirits don't care if my door is shut or phone on mute. When they have something to say, they just tap me on the shoulder!

Speaking of my girlfriend, Alexa pops in to kiss me good-bye on her way to the gym then work. She works out every day; me, not so much. Aside from a morning donut, I do try to eat healthy, but Alexa has a better chance of seeing Christ at the gym than me. Last year she convinced me to join for a few months, but when she saw I only joined to use the tanning beds, she knew it was a lost cause.

Suddenly I get another message from beyond—a new soul is in the room. An older woman who, based on the signal I'm getting, died of cancer. It appears she desperately wants to clear up some misunderstanding. Spirit is always happy to provide closure and clarity to the living. Sometime today I will likely be delivering a healing message courtesy of my latest visitor. It never ceases to amaze me how spirits show up even before my clients do!

CLEARING UP MISCONCEPTIONS

My calendar pings to tell me it's time for the day's first reading. These days I do all readings via phone or Skype—no more clients at home. Technology enables me to help more people wherever they might live. I might Skype with someone in Tennessee, followed by a client in Japan. Clients seem more relaxed when they can consult with me from their own home, and I can focus 100 percent on their spirit messages. This leads me to a frequent question: *Can you give a good reading over the phone or Skype?* Actually, I give a much better reading! Psychics who insist on seeing you in person are tuning in to you, not your spirit. They're observing your reactions to their reading or looking for clues from your body, clothes, or jewelry.

When I *read* a client, I focus on the soul coming through. Some people say mediums should not ask leading questions. I wish I had time! I barely have time to get the departed's name, cause of death, and message. I generally hear and feel the soul before I get on the phone. Once I'm actually speaking with my client via phone or Skype, things get even clearer. Souls on the other side have so much to say and come through at such a quick vibration, I have to work hard to catch everything they wish to impart. Forget about asking questions! I listen with eyes closed and work hard to capture the full meaning. If you have watched some of my videos, you will know what I am talking about. The moment I connect with a soul, information follows. I talk quickly because I get so excited to tell the person what their loved one is saying. Not to mention how fast the spirits speak. It can be very draining on my energy.

My elderly lady from the other side is nudging me. I have a feeling the time has come to help her clear up some unfinished business and give my first client of the day some clarity and healing.

My first client Skypes in and I immediately see her mom standing with her in spirit. It was the same spirit who was trying to reach me all morning.

"Your mother is here waiting for you," I assure my client. "She wants to clear something up."

My spirit visitor confirms the tingling feeling that she had cancer.

"Your mother died of cancer."

"No, no." My client sounds agitated. "You must be talking to someone else. My mother was murdered!"

I describe the mother whose spirit insists she died of brain cancer, which my physical feelings confirm. My client is crying now.

"She did have cancer, but that's not how she died. She was murdered."

Now I'm confused. Finally I learn my client couldn't accept her mother's inoperable brain cancer. She believed the hospice nurse killed her. Her mother's spirit needed to clear up this misconception so her daughter could heal. Unable to talk, eat, or swallow by the end, the woman was desperate for her daughter to know she wasn't murdered but had died of cancer and was no longer in pain. She needed her daughter to know that hospice wasn't murder, it was the right decision to allow her to be comfortable and enjoy the last few moments of her life.

Many clients suffer needlessly from similar misconceptions, memories clouded by the emotional charge of a loved one's passing. Our minds play tricks on us and we often get stuck in a belief or memory that just isn't true.

After taking a few moments to absorb this message from her mother—and shedding a few tears—my client thanks me. "It was so easy to be angry at the hospice nurse and blame her for everything. It's time to let that go. I needed to hear this from my mom today."

I have a few minutes between Skype calls. I don't know much about my next client, and I'm not getting any previews. The young man who was so persistent earlier is quiet now. I don't think he will be coming through on my next call.

THERE IS NO RETURN TO SENDER IN HEAVEN

I see a middle-aged man on my Skype screen and standing next to him is a man in spirit that looks almost identical to him. "Did you lose your brother?" I ask. Ben explains that he was not sure; he and his twin were separated at birth. For years he'd been obsessed with finding his brother but didn't have a name to go on. His adoptive parents, who'd given him a loving home, had recently passed. All he had was his deceased birth father's name.

"I'm all alone in the world but feel there's a part of me out there. I need to find my brother."

I am able to bring through his birth father, who expresses regret at not being there for his boys. I listen as his father in spirit tells me . . .

I've been watching over Ben. I need to let him know his brother Joseph died in a car accident a few months ago and is here with me. I need him to know that I am sorry I didn't help reconnect them when I was alive, but I want his heart to be at peace knowing he can stop searching.

I know how disappointed Ben will be at the news that he isn't going to be reuniting with his brother in this lifetime, but I'm obliged to share messages spirits have entrusted me with *sans* edit or filter. Altering messages to tell clients what you think they want to hear compromises your integrity as a medium. It can be a slippery slope.

After the initial shock wears off, Ben takes the news of his brother's passing surprisingly well. He is sad to know his twin had passed, but grateful for the closure.

"I had to know the truth. Otherwise I would never have stopped looking."

I would have felt better telling Ben his brother had died if I'd been able to bring through a direct message from Joseph himself, but it doesn't always work that way. I can make a request, but I can never guarantee who will come through. When you dial a number, you can't guarantee who will pick up. Sometimes no one picks up. There are many reasons. Sometimes my client is in too much grief to receive the message. Other times it's too soon; the soul hasn't completed their life review—the recently departed need time to settle in. It's much like moving into a new home; people need to unpack and set up their new home before they have visitors. We have to be patient until they're ready.

Disappointing or sensitive messages don't always go over as well as Ben's. Maybe I need a sign that reads I'M ONLY THE MESSENGER! I was doing a reading for a mother whose teenager had committed suicide. Her son came right through and told me how he'd died. He'd been very depressed and had been combining alcohol with prescription meds for depression and anxiety. He said he knew he wasn't taking his care seriously and wasn't cooperating with his mother. She was trying everything she could to get him help, but he wasn't in his right frame of mind and tragically, he hung himself.

His mother interrupted as I was sharing this. "Does he regret killing himself?"

"He does regret ending his life and wishes he had toughed it out and faced his problems instead of running from them. Now that he is on the other side, he can see how drugs had affected him, and that there were other options."

Oh my God! That poor mother freaked out. What she wanted to hear was that her son's death was inevitable—that it was his time to go and he was in the right place. To know that he had regrets and his painful death could possibly have been avoided was not comforting to her. The son was able to look back (as they say, hindsight is twenty-twenty) and see the situation more clearly. When I asked if he had regrets, I had to relay his answer no matter how painful it was for his mother to hear. In the end she accepted the message, knowing that her son was finally at peace.

When parents lose a child, they lose more than a relationship. These parents relive their loss over and over every time they watch other parents experience milestones with their children—graduations, weddings, grandchildren—they will never have with their own child.

I'M BLESSED TO BE DOING THIS WORK!

I have a few more readings, then it's time to start preparing for an evening event. Once I realized I had the ability to connect with souls on the other side, it wasn't long before I was booked solid with private readings. I soon realized group events were the perfect way to reach more people, but they take a lot of coordination and planning. Like with any career, there are many details to take care of besides the actual work you love.

Mediumship has changed a lot with technology. Skype and social media make it easier to build a community. The way I work enables me to connect a lot of people with their departed loved ones, and I'm always coming up with new ideas! But there are plenty of mediums who do it the old-fashioned way. When people learn I'm a medium, they ask what tearoom I work out of or if I have a psychic shop. Boston has cool psychic tearooms where they give you a menu. You select a drink, a psychic or medium, and the kind of reading you want. That's not my method. I started out giving readings in the back room of a hair salon, then graduated to Skype readings from home and live group reading events at hotels and auditoriums.

My sister recently told me about a business course she was taking. She laughed when I asked if she had any questions about running a business.

"What you do isn't a business. You just talk on the phone all day!"

I admit my business is a little unusual and unique, but it is a business. Like any business owner, I have to juggle schedules, plan and coordinate activities, and make sure clients have positive experiences.

SPIRIT CAN'T GIVE YOU ALL THE ANSWERS

I check a couple of emails and voice messages in my home office before I head upstairs to get ready for tonight's event. I have a two-year-long waiting list for readings, so it won't be long before my only readings will be in group settings.

One call is from a woman who wants another reading. I'm going to turn her down. Some people become addicted to psychic readings, so I try to do no more than one reading a year for my clients. When people obsess, I try to get them to focus their energy on living. You might think your departed loved one has all the answers. Maybe they do. But we're meant to overcome most challenges and obstacles ourselves. The spirit world is not there to guide us step-by-step through life, and not every challenge can be avoided. Some challenges are put into your life to make you stronger and wiser.

Sometimes I get funny questions. A woman came to me with a dilemma.

"I'm planning to get a boob job. Ask my dad if I should get a B or a C cup."

I had to explain to her that your loved ones in heaven are there to love and support you. They are not there to make decisions for you. It's your life and you are in charge of your own happiness and choices. Instead of listening, she just rephrased the question and asked:

"Okay. Instead, ask my dad if I would like the results."

Her father came through. He said she should do what made her happy, not change herself for other people.

She really wanted more concrete information, but I told her this wasn't something for the other side to determine. She had to figure this one out herself.

People often ask paternity questions. Sometimes I wonder if they think I'm Jerry Springer. In my experience, this question only gets a direct answer if there is good reason. For example, I had a call from a pregnant teenager whose ex had died in a car accident.

She wanted to know if her ex or her current boyfriend was the father. The ex-boyfriend's parents blamed her and the breakup for his accident. She wanted to tell them they were going to have a grandchild, but she was afraid of opening old wounds. The boyfriend came right through and said the baby was his. She reconnected with the family, who took it as a sign to support one another. The message I relayed helped them come together and heal, and gave the new baby grandparents, who confirmed my reading with a DNA test.

My work is never boring. I might be faced with questions about a suicide, a boob job, or who the father of a baby is—all in one day. The souls I connect with tell me the message that I will relay, and they won't share an answer that isn't helpful.

Sometimes mediums team up with the departed to play the role of therapist and help people heal, but regular therapy is important, too. You might feel like you're still able to talk to someone you miss by talking to a medium, but that isn't what is meant to be. Yes, your loved one is still with you in spirit, but it's important to get on with your own life. It's important to find the right balance. Too much dependence on readings and connecting to the other side can disturb that balance.

IF IT'S TUESDAY, IT MUST BE THE MARRIOTT

I start laying out my clothes for tonight's live event. It's fun to express my personal style onstage. It's fun to wear unique clothing others are afraid to wear. I love things that reveal my personality—

shoes with crystals, for instance. Actually, I wear my *stage clothes* almost everywhere I go!

Check out my events page. You'll see I do several events a week. Right now audiences are limited, but that's changing soon. I'll be doing bigger events to accommodate the many people who want to be part of the experience of proving that there is an afterlife. I hate to turn people away!

These days most of these events are within a fifty-mile radius of my home. Rhode Islanders are notorious for refusing to drive more than twenty-five miles for a job, concert, significant other, whatever. But as my reputation grows, I've started to branch out with events as far away as Arizona and California. Maybe I'm not really a Rhode Islander after all!

I get to the hotel early for tonight's event. People are starting to line up outside, and I go into the hall for a sound check. The lighting looks fine and the hotel has lined up chairs theater-style. The doors are still closed, but the souls are already gathering! I see the young man who had showed up this morning. He'll likely be one of the first readings tonight. I say a quick prayer as I walk around the room, and then it's time to open the doors.

The crowd enters. After a little intro, it's off to the races! There will be two hours of solid readings. As I look out at the audience, I see those in spirit right behind them. I let people know what to expect but try not to talk about myself too much. That is not what they're here for. I walk into the crowd and immediately start connecting. Your loved one might be right behind you as you sit in the audience! I check the room. Some people have one soul with them; others a whole family group. I might read anywhere from twenty-five to fifty audience members, but hundreds of spirits typically come through in a night.

I do as many readings as I can, but can't read everyone in the audience. The good news is that many readings give insight to other audience members.

NO ONE GOES AWAY EMPTY-HANDED

I used to worry about disappointing those who attend an event but don't get a reading. Not anymore. My mother helps out—she sells my books, T-shirts, and jewelry at events. Often she is the first person people meet at my events. Sometimes people tell her they'll be mad if they don't get a reading! Then on the way out they stop to tell her how much the experience meant to them—even if they didn't get a direct message.

Heaven has a way of giving people what they need. They learn so much from others' readings. The most important takeaway? Proof there is an afterlife, and that your loved ones are only a thought away.

Tonight the young man who overdosed is first up, standing behind a woman. He says something about being a boyfriend.

I look at the woman and say, "I have a boyfriend coming through for you."

The woman looks confused. She's married, but it soon becomes clear I'm connecting with her stepdaughter's boyfriend who died of an overdose. The girl, who'd been going through rehab, was fighting with her boyfriend when he died. At the time he didn't want to get clean. Now he was desperate to send a message of apology. The stepmother was surprised he would come through to her—they were never close. But he was coming through to warn the stepmother that her stepdaughter was lost and in pain and dangerously close to losing what she'd gained in rehab. His soul was so persistent because he knew connecting with her stepmother was the only way to warn the family their daughter was struggling. Spirit will make it through the smallest opening if the message is important.

After twenty more readings and signing autographs, I'm drained—and starving. I'm obsessed with The Cheesecake Factory and love to go there with Mom and Alexa after an event—their menu is so varied. People recognize me; some were even at my event. Several fans stop by our table and I sign a few autographs while we wait for our dinner. I always save room for cheesecake—usually the vanilla bean, cinnamon bun, or cookie dough.

SUGGESTED VIDEO: Google "Psychic Medium Matt Fraser Reads Audience Members" to watch inspirational readings from one of my live events. I hope as you watch, you can relate to the messages and feel closer to your own family members in spirit.

TOOLS FOR LIFE

I depend on my daily rituals to help me start the morning off right and stay focused and on track all day long! I believe these simple habits free my mind to receive messages from souls in heaven.

If you'd like to tap into your spiritual side or simply get through your own busy day with mindfulness, balance, and a dash of fun, I encourage you to incorporate some of these simple habits into your schedule.

Let the music move you: I start each day listening to happy, upbeat music—I have my special disco mix for mornings and another mellower playlist for when I'm traveling to an event. You can create your own personal soundtrack for every occasion. Try labeling playlists for morning, drive time, relaxation, exercise. Any activity you love can be made a little better with the right tunes!

Tune out and tune in: Incorporate meditation or quiet time into your day, and if you think you're too busy to meditate, think again! Taking just five minutes to sit and let your mind be still is like pushing some kind of internal reset button. When you're done, you'll feel calm, refreshed, and ready to tackle the day.

Keep a calendar: I always say that when it's on my calendar, it's off my mind! With so many events, media appearances, and other commitments, having everything in a single location helps me to prepare for what's ahead and block out time for family and friends. Personally, I like my paper planner, but there are lots of great options for your computer and smartphone too.

Don't get pulled off course: When I'm in work mode, I do everything I can to stay on task and try to limit interruptions. Only after I've gotten through most of my to-do list do I check emails and voice messages. I can't stress enough how that habit helps me stay focused and accomplish more every single day. It can work for you too.

Come from a place of gratitude: Feeling overwhelmed? Take a minute to count your blessings. Sometimes I feel like my schedule is too much for any one person, but then I remember how blessed I am to be doing meaningful work that I love, and suddenly I find myself tackling my to-do list with a smile.

Above everything, be kind: Kindness is the energy I try to maintain every day. Even when someone is being difficult or demanding, I put myself in their shoes and try to understand where they're coming from. It's better for everyone involved, especially me, because it's a whole lot easier to deal with people when you come from a place of compassion rather than judgment.

Make time for what matters most: If my evenings are not spent at events, you can usually find me breaking bread with my family. I love to share a meal (and cheesecake) with Alexa and my parents, and often extended family and friends join us. I cherish these times; connecting with those I love is so precious to me. Building new memories or sharing happy stories about loved ones here and in heaven nourishes the spirit in the best way possible.

CHAPTER 2

The Early Years or "Doesn't Everyone See Ghosts?"

People always ask how old I was when I realized I was a medium. You might assume being able to connect with the dead is like any other gift. It's not. Imagine you had a special talent—pitching a baseball, playing the piano, learning languages. Chances are parents and teachers would discover this talent at an early age and you'd practice and take lessons and just get better and better. Hopefully, adults in your life would support and encourage you so you could play ball, become a concert pianist, or perhaps a UN translator.

I've turned my gift into a career, but the path wasn't that straightforward. There were definitely some challenges along the way, but I'm blessed to have ultimately been given the guidance and support I needed to be where I am today.

Between the age of three and four years old I realized I could hear ghosts. I thought I was being haunted, and naturally I was afraid. The more I tried not to see these scary images, the closer they came and the louder they got! Throughout my childhood I had an awareness of spirits around me but didn't really understand what was going on. Talking about it produced mixed reactions from parents, teachers, and other kids. By mixed I mean they were sure I was just imagining it! So I stopped sharing and pushed my gift away until the visions and voices slowed down and disappeared entirely during my teen years.

To explain how I finally accepted my gift, I'd better start at the beginning.

MESSAGES FROM GRANDMA

My dad was in the navy when I was born, so he was deployed a lot while I was growing up. Mom and I moved in with my grandparents. Mom worked full-time. So did Grandpa, whom I know as "Poppy."

Most of the time it was just me and Grandma Mary, who just so happened to be psychic. Because being psychic was such a controversy in those days, my grandfather never knew about my grandmother's psychic gift. She did her best to hide it from him and would only bring out her cards with select friends and family members while Poppy was at work or away.

She was very loving and took great care of me, so naturally I was very attached to her.

When I was just about three, Grandma Mary passed. A bereavement counselor advised Mom to bring me to the wake so I'd have closure. It didn't work. She didn't feel any different to me because I was still feeling the same connection. I was confused. I didn't realize she had passed and told her to get out of the box. At three I just didn't understand what was going on and was upset at having to leave her body behind. How could we go home without Grandma? Being so young, all I remember was everyone leaving the funeral parlor and not having my Grandma there. In the end it didn't matter. At night Grandma would show up in spirit at the foot of my bed and wake me up. One time she led me into the living room and read to me just like when she was alive.

I have a clear memory of Grandma appearing to me after she passed, wearing the long white dress she'd been buried in. Mom and I were getting ready to move and had been packing boxes all day. After Mom went to bed, Grandma showed up. I remember I was sitting on her lap as the angels sat on moving boxes all around us. It sounds funny but it was really comforting for a lonely little boy who missed his grandma.

I was too young to really understand what was going on. I'd tell Mom what was happening, but she missed her mother too much herself and was too distracted to pay much attention, which was kind of ironic since Mom was also psychic. In fact, before Grandma died, Mom begged her to come back and visit.

Later Mom told me her mother said, *If I can I will. If not, I'll send signs, so watch out for them!*

When she passed over, my grandmother never did visit my mother. Instead she visited me. I told Mom, but grief prevented her from really getting it until I started telling others. They told her, and then she started paying attention.

One day I woke up with a message from Grandma for her daughter. She said Mom was drowning in grief and needed to let go.

Please tell your mom she has a family to take care of and to please move on and live her life. She has too much to live for and can't let me hold her back.

I asked Grandma why she couldn't tell Mom herself. She said it wouldn't be good for the family. Mom had always relied on Grandma for everything and she might get too caught up trying to connect with her in spirit.

I don't remember a lot about what happened when I shared this. I do remember Mom crying. I was happy she finally heard me and accepted the message.

It was not in the least scary to have Grandma come through. I found it comforting and wonderful. What came next was not so wonderful.

GET ME OUT OF HERE— THIS PLACE IS HAUNTED!

When Grandma's visits slowed down other souls began coming through. This scared the heck out of me. I would hear whispers around me and see strangers or dark shadows at the foot of my bed. They were so scary! I'd open my eyes and see a shadow, then suddenly the figure of a man. The whispers would get louder and louder. I'd scream like crazy and make Mom lie down next to me until I fell asleep. I think I tried to sleep with my parents until I was thirteen! I was just so afraid.

Soon I was experiencing these encounters whenever I was alone. I'd be in my basement playroom and hear voices—sometimes someone familiar like Mom or Grandpa calling my name. But the person calling me was either fast asleep or not at home.

One time Dad was home. I was playing by myself downstairs. I had always loved my playroom and spent a lot of time there. I was happily puttering around with my karaoke machine, listening to Radio Disney. Suddenly I heard a man's voice yelling through the speaker. I ran upstairs and made Dad go down and turn the karaoke machine off.

The visions and voices would only come through if I were alone in my room or the playroom, never in the street or the schoolyard. I didn't realize I was psychic. I just thought the house was haunted. I told Mom, *There's something wrong with this house. I want to move.* It only got worse. I had no idea ignoring the voices made them more determined to get my attention. It's funny. Once I accepted my gift, I could go back to my grandparents' house with no problem. It's clean and not haunted at all. But at the time, I drove Dad nuts with my fear of the dark. I insisted on sleeping with the lights on and the TV blaring to drown out the whispers. Dad did everything he could. He installed night-lights, as if a little night-light would do anything. What I needed were floodlights that would light up my room like an airport!

He finally gave up and started turning everything off before he went to bed. Sometimes I could sleep through the night but many nights I woke up to whispers, and then I woke up the whole family.

MOM TO THE RESCUE

When I started kindergarten, I had a hard time fitting in at school because I was telling the kids and the teacher I saw spirits and my grandmother came to visit. Like any child, I would ramble on about whatever crossed my mind, and this was a big deal. I was obsessed with talking about it.

Everyone thought it was my imagination, but eventually my "ghost stories" got out of hand and started scaring the other kids. My teacher called Mom in. She suggested I see a child psychologist. Mom was conflicted. She was psychic and understood what I was going through to a point, but she was in and out of denial. Teachers and relatives and Dad did not understand at all. Still grieving her mother, Mom was stuck in the middle with a psychic kid and no idea what to do.

Off I went to the child psychologist. She played games with me and asked about Grandma. I liked playing with new toys and having an adult pay so much attention to me. I had no idea she was planning to put me on meds.

The psychologist was convinced I was making it all up because of a desperate need for Grandma to be alive. This never rang quite true to Mom who, listening to the psychologist explain away my visions as a little boy's wishful thinking, realized the exact opposite was true. The psychologist finally started to listen more when I talked about the voices and visions, and started asking questions that proved I was truly seeing and hearing and experiencing things psychically.

By the time the psychologist tried to put me on all kinds of medications, Mom had gotten over her denial and was ready to take matters into her own hands. She canceled the sessions and started to ask me very specific evidential questions to help figure out who was speaking.

What is she wearing?

What do the voices say?

AN IMPORTANT JOB
FOR A YOUNG MEDIUM

When you are psychic, souls who have passed know they can come to you to transmit messages to loved ones. They don't bother those who can't see or hear them. They communicate with those connected to where they spent time when they were alive. Mom always felt it was the medium's duty to relay these messages so that the soul could be at peace. She told me not to be afraid. She would stand right next to the ghosts and show me they weren't hurting her. She said she'd had the same visions as a child and Grandma had comforted her the same way.

She told me to listen to the messages. They were important. They were souls who had passed—neighbors and people who had worked nearby. She begged me to listen. I still couldn't or wouldn't, but having Mom believe me and try to help me made it a lot easier to deal what was happening.

LIVING WITH MY GIFT

After Grandma Mary passed, we left my grandparents' house. Dad's navy career required moving around a lot. At age six we were living in Mississippi when Hurricane Danny forced us to evacuate. Dad was out at sea. We were alone and scared in a hotel. We were all in bed sleeping, waiting for the storm to pass, when suddenly my mom noticed the *sickness smell* she'd sensed when Grandma lay dying. Mom knew immediately that Grandma was there in spirit. She looked over to me in the next bed, and I started sleep-talking to someone. Mom knew it was her mother and wanted to know what she was saying. I said Grandma Mary is here; she's asking me to move over so she could lie on the couch and comfort me. She didn't want the thunder and lightning to scare me. My mom knew instantly that her mother was there to help us brave the storm.

GROWING UP PSYCHIC

You might wonder why Mom took so long to fully accept she was raising a psychic medium. Even though she and her mother both had the gift, Mom never went to mediums or psychics or watched them on TV. They weren't as popular as they are now—at least not in our neighborhood. We'd never heard of John Edward or James Van Praagh or other mediums.

As a child I didn't know not to tell people about the ghosts and visions I saw. I was trying to live a normal life. As I got older, I succeeded at pushing the visions and voices away for the most part, and at some point they started to subside. To be completely honest, I forgot about them. Kids are like that! I felt the voices were just a phase of life that was now over. Keep in mind I still really thought that old house was haunted. I didn't connect it with me.

I wanted to meet someone who understood, a best friend with similar abilities. I never met anyone like that. Instead I was drawn to Harry Potter books and movies, and TV shows like *That's So Raven*, where kids had paranormal skills.

IS MY CHILD PSYCHIC?

These days there's more of an awareness of kids with special gifts. Some parents seem eager to pick up on the smallest hint of the paranormal and push their kids to be psychics and mediums. I think it's important to be open to what's happening, but there's a difference between being open and accepting and pushing something on your kids.

Personally, I've not had direct contact with psychic kids, though parents often approach me with requests for advice with regard to a child who may be psychic.

Here's what I say: *Hear them out. Listen to your child's experience as they ramble on and describe visions and/or voices. Ask the right questions—for instance, who do they see? Ask how many times this has happened and how it makes them feel—sad, happy, indifferent, afraid?*

Make mental notes as you listen. Is your child referring to an imaginary friend or a loved one in heaven?

Observe how your child plays alone. Do they talk to themselves; prefer to be alone; get along with other children?

Show your child pictures of departed loved ones and ask if that's who they're seeing. Explain who that person is and let them know they are like an angel.

Ask other family members, teachers, and caregivers if they've observed the same behavior when you are not there.

Avoid leading questions. Instead, casually ask who they're talking to; why are they afraid; what are they seeing; why can't I see them too; and has this happened before?

Comfort, support, and validate your child.

KEEPING THE PSYCHIC CONNECTION

One thing that I will say is that children are born with a close, natural connection to spirit. It's common for them to have paranormal experiences like receiving psychic messages or seeing visions. The younger they are, the more accepting they are of these incidents. As they get older, fear and the desire to fit in and be "normal" become more important, so they tend to distance themselves from their gifts. The rare children who are able to maintain their connection through their teenage years and beyond, or who rediscover their abilities as adults, are the people whom we consider to be psychics or mediums and many times, like in my case, it runs in the family.

GIFTED CHILDREN COME IN MANY VARIETIES

You may have heard people talk about *Crystal children*, *Indigo children*, and *Rainbow children*—terms for special types of gifted children. Here are some descriptions of how these children might behave, as well as how they can best use their gifts, and how to best support and nurture these special children.

Indigo Children

Indigo children always seem to make waves. They do not accept authority and are intuitive, psychic, creative, and fearless. They can get frustrated and be insecure. They need an environment with clear boundaries and structure to feel safe growing up. With the proper guidance and nurturing, they will grow up to challenge tradition and help open the world to new ways of thinking.

These children often grow up to be successful business leaders, politicians, and critical thinkers. The downside is that they do not learn the same way as others, and often grow bored with regular schooling and require more hands-on learning environments.

Crystal Children

Crystal children are healers in touch with their own energy and happy to share it with those around them. They usually have a parent who is an Indigo adult. Crystal children are emotional and make decisions based on intuition and feeling rather than just the facts. They are great at connecting with young children, animals, and vulnerable people. They are born comforters.

Crystal children grow up to be great doctors, nurses, and counselors. Some grow up to be veterinarians, massage therapists, or even schoolteachers. They have a strong intuitive sense.

Rainbow Children

Rainbow children are sometimes referred to as *new souls*. They usually have a parent who is a Crystal adult, so at least one parent will understand them. They may be threatening to others because people are resistant to their visions and actions. Rainbow children are brave, loving, and strong. They cannot be contained. They are often telepathic and march to their own beat, unconcerned about what other people think of them.

Rainbow children like to spend time alone. They absorb new ideas and teachings quickly. They are well-rounded and can change hobbies, or friends, quickly. They love travel and adventure, and are very creative and artistic.

Rainbow children grow up to be great marketers, inventors, and managers. They love setting goals and working to achieve them. They prefer to work in the background, happy to be a silent partner or backbone standing behind a growing company or leader.

Remember, children who seem different are not bad or in need of medication, just different. When a child talks about his or her vision of the future or some idea that seems, well, crazy, stop for a moment and just listen. You may be in the presence of a child with psychic gifts; gifts that can help the world.

Where Were You When I Was Growing Up?

I would have loved a friend who understood me when I was growing up, but I never met another psychic kid until I was a teenager.

By the time I went to EMT school, I had stopped trying to shut out spirit and had opened up. I was starting to talk about it again. I was lucky to team up with another EMT trainee who was psychic too. She told me she'd had similar experiences as a child—including visions! She told me she'd sensed I could also communicate with the dead. I was just starting to accept the messages and even do a few readings. For her, she said it took too much energy out of her and gave her a headache. We'd both been drawn to a career as an EMT because we wanted to help and heal people. Her gifts made her a natural at helping people who were hurt, scared, and sometimes dying.

If I'd known her as a child, life would have been a lot easier! It was the first time that I realized that I was not alone. It was at this moment that I realized I had a gift and I had no choice but to run with it. I realized that the more I shared my story, the more accepting people were. Many had their own stories, and some even had their own ability. Although my EMT friend never embraced her gift of delivering messages, she embraced her abilities in another way—helping people heal with her medical intuitive abilities.

I felt this gift was given to me for a deeper reason. It showed me that I was missing my calling, and that I had to help people on a much deeper level. I was meant to deliver messages from those they love and lost. I didn't feel alone anymore, and I was ready to come out of hiding and embrace my own psychic gift.

SUGGESTED VIDEO: Google "Matt Fraser Spine Tingling Psychic Reading" to watch a mini behind-the-scenes special of my life growing up psychic. My mom is also in the video, sharing her story of when I was born.

TOOLS FOR LIFE

I started this chapter by explaining how parents can nurture their child's special gift, whatever it might be. This becomes a little trickier if your child's special ability happens to be talking to dead people, because schools, camps, clubs, and lessons that cater to psychic and mediumistic kids are few and far between.

Being a supportive parent means being alert and aware of your child's interests. Watch him as he does his homework, plays with his friends. Pay attention to the shows he likes to watch and the books he likes to read. Notice what lights him up and makes him smile.

Be careful not to let your own passion, or what you think is "best" for your child, cloud your vision. By all means, expose your child to lots of different things, but try not to impose your dreams on him or her.

Everyone's different. Not every child will love technology, some would rather paint or play outside or spend time with animals. Some children will pursue the same passion their entire life, while others might want to learn lots of new skills and try lots of hobbies.

Your child might grow up to be an artist, a salesperson, a mechanic, an architect, an actor, or a writer. They might pursue a career in politics or public service.

We are all given gifts from heaven, and most parents are eager to help their child accept, grow, and share their gift. As you encourage your child, you will also strengthen your bond with them.

And it's not all about the kids! As a parent, pay attention to your own passion. Remember what you loved as a child, and spend some time on that activity, with or without your child. Be as supportive of yourself as you are of your child. Open your mind. Who knows what new opportunities and experiences might present themselves to you?

CHAPTER 3

High School Hell

Everyone asks me, is there a hell? Yes. It's right here on earth and it's called high school!

To say that high school was difficult is an understatement, but I wouldn't be where I am today without lessons learned there. There are blessings to be found in even the most difficult circumstances.

People assume that I didn't fit in with the high school crowd because I speak to dead people. That was the least of my problems. And for most of my high school years, no one knew about that side of my life. I'd pushed it away to the point that I'd almost forgotten I even had psychic abilities.

HIGH SCHOOL IS NO PLACE FOR A SENSITIVE SOUL

My family moved to Boston right about when I was starting high school because my father was appointed fire commissioner for the

City of Boston. Dad asked around the office to find the best school for his son. My parents wanted the best for me, but the expensive and prestigious prep school they finally chose could not have been a worse fit!

In high school I was very sensitive. I didn't do readings, but I was definitely different from the other kids. I guess I was an old soul who couldn't relate to things my classmates cared about. Nothing about me fit in. For example, I've always had a strong work ethic and enjoy helping people. I also love style and fashion. From a young age I held multiple jobs. My classmates were country club lifeguards or caddies. They thought my jobs—working for the City of Boston, as a camp counselor, or selling clothes at Abercrombie & Fitch—were weird.

My lack of athletic ability was an even bigger issue. We soon discovered the school's mission was to groom students for sports scholarships. Not a good place for the least athletic person you will ever meet. Everything revolved around sports, and the first thing kids asked me was if I played hockey.

But I had a bigger problem. Many of the kids were the sons of firemen. My dad was their boss during a time when there were major disputes with the union, which didn't make Dad popular with the firemen. It wasn't an easy time for him. He was too stressed for me to bother him with my problems and tell him that his job was spilling into my school life.

At home, kids heard their dads complain about the new commissioner, so they would come to school and take it out on me. Unless they were bullying me, they didn't talk to me at all. I didn't have a single friend. If I'd liked to drink or smoke, I might have made friends at parties. If I was an athlete, we might have worked things out on the basketball court or the baseball field. But that wasn't me and I remained an outcast.

A lot of high school was a blur. I was diagnosed with anxiety and was convinced I was bringing it upon myself. I signed up for an extra language course and hung out in the library to avoid the agony of eating lunch alone. For three years I plowed through, counting the days until graduation. My parents were spending a fortune to send me to a place they thought was best for me. I didn't have the heart to tell them why it was making me miserable.

I started to hear stories about bullying and how it was leading to a record number of kid suicides. I didn't want to wind up a statistic and realized I needed to come clean with my parents. It was hard! I wanted to make my parents proud, not think their sacrifices were for nothing. But watching news stories about teen suicide scared me. I knew something had to change. I talked to my parents and they weren't happy, but they agreed to let me start senior year in a new public school.

A WHOLE NEW WORLD

The contrast between public school and that fancy prep school was night and day. No one at the new school knew who my father was, nor did they care. There were parties and sports but also lots of other activities. I quickly found a group of friends.

My new school was very laid-back, with little pressure to excel at sports and impress college recruiters. I could finally be myself. I could dress up and dance and be part of the teen nightlife. I met other kids who liked that too, and started organizing under-21 nights with a limo company at the club. Suddenly I was meeting new people and felt accepted for who I was. I was having a great time.

That experience taught me something important. For three years I beat myself up because I didn't fit the mold. We encourage kids to be accountable and tough it out when the going gets rough, but sometimes you need to be aware enough to say *this isn't working* and make a change. That can take as much strength and account-ability as toughing things out.

Now I can look back and see the problem with prep school wasn't me. It just wasn't a fit. But I don't regret those three years of feeling alone and disconnected. They helped me better under-stand people who are sad and grieving. High school was a blessing because it ultimately taught me empathy.

I could deny my mediumship throughout my teens, but not my sensitive side. I believe that experience with bullying helped me become the medium I am today.

FINDING MY DREAM JOB

Those difficult years made me realize I wanted a career in which I could help people. First, I thought I'd be a therapist. I knew I could make a difference, given my own experience and insight into people, which I didn't realize was tied to my psychic abilities. Then I thought about becoming an EMT and helping people who were injured began to make sense. I started taking classes and working toward becoming an EMT.

Before I knew it, I was graduating from high school and on the road to a career. I had some questions about where my EMT studies would lead and couldn't decide whether to become an EMT or a paramedic. As I was trying to figure out my next step, I heard about a well-known psychic working out of a local tearoom. I thought she might be able to offer some guidance on my career path, and tell me my chances with a girl I liked.

The psychic wasn't interested in my questions because she immediately picked up on my childhood experiences. Suddenly my grandma Mary came through and told the psychic that she'd spoken to me as a child after she'd passed, and I was as psychic as she was. The medium started telling me everything my grandma was saying. I wasn't expecting this, and it threw me for a loop. I told her I didn't hear things anymore. She said I'd shut down and needed to embrace my ability.

I didn't want to hear that. All I wanted were answers to my questions. *What about the girl? My career?* I was not happy with her reading. I wanted to hear I was destined to be an EMT. She told me I was a medium. I wanted my money back.

The psychic was firm. *Go home and meditate. Focus on a white light coming out of your forehead. Ask your gift to return.* For some reason I did as she suggested, and the whispers returned. Messages flooded in from all sorts of souls. I couldn't wait to come out of my meditative state and share them, but as it turned out, I couldn't remember even one message or vision. It didn't matter. I was open and awake again. My life had totally changed.

FROM THE BACK ROOM OF
A HAIR SALON TO THE MORNING NEWS!

After I went to the medium, I started doing readings for friends—if you could call them readings! Those early messages were much different and lighter than they are now. It was kind of like a teenage game, a party trick. I had no idea of the power behind the gift I was using to make predictions. We were teenagers who wanted to know answers to teenage questions. Occasionally a grandmother or great uncle in spirit would make an appearance, but mostly it was simple fluffy stuff. I started giving little readings for ten dollars in the back of a hair salon, then people hired me to read for groups.

Looking back, things changed once I started doing house parties for more mature clients—adults who had lost loved ones or wanted to know about surgeries and divorces. As the messages got weightier than who was going to the prom with whom or what college we were going to, I changed. Empathy kicked in. I began to feel people's pain. I realized being a medium meant acting as a psychic and a counselor. I needed to use my gift for serious questions in order to be taken seriously. I wasn't a mind reader or a fortune-teller. I wanted to spend my life helping and healing people. As it turned out, my original career goal was on the money.

MESSAGES FROM UNEXPECTED PLACES

One incident around this time really opened my eyes to what my gift might mean to other people. I was helping a friend move into her college dorm room—nothing unusual. Walking into her room I noticed a big collage of photos of friends and relatives. My attention was drawn to a beautiful headshot of a man. Suddenly the photo appeared to spring to life and he started talking to me.

He said he'd been like a father to my friend but felt bad he hadn't spoken to her much when she got older. They still cared about each other, but life had just gotten in the way. Looking back he regretted not spending more time with her. Most of their memories were from when she was a very young child. He'd always thought they'd have more time, but he'd died unexpectedly in a plane crash.

I had no idea what to do with this information. I was new to my gift and didn't know what to say. Was I just imagining it? How could I bring up something like this with my friend who was happily decorating her new room? Luckily, she saw me looking at the picture and came over. I asked if the man was her father. She said no but that he'd been like a father to her. I asked if he'd died in a plane crash. She was shocked.

"Who told you that? I don't talk about him with many people."

I said he'd told me. As I relayed his message, her eyes welled up with tears. I told her how much he loved her and regretted time not spent, but that he was honored she still kept his picture with her no matter where she went. She was stunned and happy and clearly very moved by his message.

That was one of the first experiences to truly validate my gift and change my perspective. I realized I had to be open. Messages could come anytime, anywhere, even from a collage in a college dorm room. More important, I realized I didn't need to fear delivering messages that were clearly so precious to their recipient. Knowing he was watching over her as she transitioned to college gave my friend so much peace and clarity.

Word of that reading soon spread. Students and even teachers from the college started seeking me out for readings. They would line up with questions or ask me to connect with souls in heaven. Next thing I knew, their parents and their parents' friends wanted readings, too.

THERE ISN'T A SCHOOL FOR THIS?

EMT school was one thing, but who knew where to go to learn how to become a professional psychic medium? There were mediums on TV and some were holding events, but I wasn't aware of them. I realized answers would have to come from inside me and I needed to look at everything on a deeper level.

I spent a lot of time sitting quietly by myself, learning how to tune in and ask the other side for answers. It was like learning another language.

My readings got better and better. Soon I was no longer predicting prom dates. I was channeling grandmothers, appearing on TV, and making headlines. From the outside it may have looked quick and easy, but I was working hard with my clients and spending hours in self-study with mentors on the other side. In my free time I would speak to spirit guides, deceased relatives, and different souls who would answer questions about my gift.

My work left me with more questions.

Why are people taken so traumatically?

Why do we lose children?

Why can't heaven intervene when something horrible is about to happen?

I asked my spirit guides for answers, but the answer was that I needed to change my perspective. My guides explained that whether we live to be one hundred years old or pass at twelve years old, our lifetimes are like seconds compared to the eternity of heaven. It's like waiting at a stoplight. Years from now you won't remember if it was five seconds or five minutes. The time you waited is minuscule in the context of your entire life.

As my career took off and I began booking small events and local TV appearances, some of the friends I'd made toward the end of my time in high school stopped hanging out with me. But I'd been through that before and didn't worry. I had many positive people in my life and great opportunities before me.

It's hard to be different in high school. Everyone is just trying to fit in. Try fitting in when you talk to dead people. But those things that made you stick out like a sore thumb in high school might be just the ticket to success later in life. So if you're struggling to fit in, or feeling like you don't have anything to offer, hang in there!

SUGGESTED VIDEO: Google "Psychic Medium Matt Fraser LIVE Event Video" to watch footage of one of my first ever live group readings. I can't believe how young I was in this video!

TOOLS FOR LIFE

Bullying is a very serious topic. It doesn't matter if someone posts online or confronts you face-to-face, bullying comments hurt—and they can lead to depression and suicidal thoughts in children and teens. As a parent, teacher, or concerned adult you can take steps to help.

If your child is showing signs of distress, like not wanting to attend school or participate in activities that they once enjoyed, gently try to discuss the situation with them. Let them know that you are there to listen, and be careful not to say anything to discount their pain, or make them feel like their actions caused the abuse. When they're first starting to open up to you, the most important thing you can do is listen.

Once they've opened up, let your child know you understand their distress and that it is not their fault. Assure them that they do not deserve to be treated badly. Explain what steps you are about to take and acknowledge that it took courage for them to open up to you.

If your child is having trouble at school, request an in-person meeting with the principal to discuss the situation and outline steps they can take to protect your child and stop the bullying.

Don't be afraid to ask for help from the school administration. Changing your child's classes—or changing schools—to get them away from students who are hurting them might seem drastic, but this kind of action might be exactly what is needed.

You can expect discipline for the bullies; their parents should be called in to alert them that action is being taken and expulsion will be the next step. ZERO tolerance is now the law.

If the principal does not agree or follow up, explain you will be holding them liable and that you won't hesitate to take it to social media and voice your concern.

You will be surprised how quickly a school system responds.

While you're working to stop the bullying, continue to reinforce positive feedback to your child. Let them know that you are on their side, and continue to provide a safe place where they can share their feelings.

You can also find resources online. Here's just one organization that can help you: https://www.stopbullying.gov/.

CHAPTER 4

Helping and Healing

'm still fairly young, but as I look back on my life, I realize I've already taken a few big twists and turns. My goal has stayed the same. I just found a different path.

I've been hyperaware of people's suffering since childhood. I always wanted to help make folks feel better. As I got older, being an EMT seemed like a logical first step. I planned to become an EMT, then a paramedic, and finally a physician's assistant. Psychic medium wasn't on the list.

I spent one year as an EMT. I've never been afraid of death. Perhaps it's because of my connection with spirit. A feeling of calm comes over me when I'm around blood and gore. EMTs and paramedics will tell you, *Do what you have to do. Don't be afraid to break some ribs to save someone's life.* You're trained to go into a zone and do your job.

TEA AND A LIFE-CHANGING MESSAGE

I knew I wanted to keep doing this work, but all the choices, paths, and training were a bit overwhelming. I wasn't really sure what to do. So when the local psychic opened the door for me, I walked through it. But there was some overlap. I've never been afraid to work multiple jobs, so I started out slowly, continuing as an EMT while I explored my psychic mediumship.

At that time, I was working at the Seaport World Trade Center in Boston and loving it. Part convention center and part financial institution, it's a unique and busy place. It was an atypical EMT assignment without a lot of drama. It was rare that anyone came to me with a serious injury or illness; mostly I saw asthma attacks and sprained ankles and felt like a school nurse!

Ambulance-based EMTs are like FedEx. Their job is to get patients to a hospital as fast as possible. My situation was different. I had to assess people to determine if an ambulance was needed. I made full use of my EMT training and insight into people to make that judgment call. Often I sat with them and helped them through whatever was happening—for instance, a panic attack before a big meeting or an asthma attack they thought was a heart attack. The right call was critical. My patient might be attending a conference or on a family vacation. The last place they wanted to go was the hospital. Often I was able to help them avoid an unnecessary visit to the emergency room. This experience really taught me how closely our minds and bodies are linked. I was shocked to see how stress, anxiety, and fear could manifest in so many physical symptoms.

KEEPING BUSY ON THE NIGHT SHIFT

I started working at the center as a security officer. Management liked me and was very flexible with those who were willing to work hard. After I completed my EMT training, they let me be a combination EMT and security officer.

As a relatively new employee, I worked the graveyard shift from eleven p.m. to seven a.m. The convention halls were empty and the financial offices were closed. We were a small skeleton crew responsible for the hotel guests. Even with so few people working, we had very little to do. My colleagues read or napped. I built my psychic medium business! My body clock adjusted and I became a night owl who used all that free time to build my website, write my first book, and schedule and prepare for readings.

During that time I really began to develop my gift. I'd get calls during the night shift from hotel guests. I'd practice my craft on every call, honing my ability until I could predict the severity of each one. But soon, with more seniority, I was moved to the day shift. Suddenly I went from quiet nights working with ten people running the hotel, to a day shift with hundreds of employees. During the night shifts I'd eat my sandwich in an empty employee lunchroom. Now that I was on the day shift, I could barely find a seat. But I got used to it. The day shift had its own benefits.

Word soon got out among the staff that I was a medium. Day-shift employees were a little older and more accepting of my gift than my friends from high school. They came to me with questions and stories of their own paranormal experiences. Sometimes I'd do readings. I loved going to work in a place where I felt so accepted.

Feeling that people understand and like the real you does wonders for your mood!

WHO'S THAT LITTLE BLOND GIRL?

During my time at Seaport, my boss invited me to his house for a family Christmas gathering. As soon as I got there, I saw a little blond girl run by in spirit. She was wearing a white communion-style dress and holding a little Yorkie. I shared my vision with the group, who laughed because they had no little blond girls in the family. My boss used to tease me about it at work. *Remember the little blond girl?*

Later that holiday season, my boss showed me a photo he'd taken of their Christmas tree, which showed the little girl and her dog sitting at the base of the tree. Here is the photo he took. If you look closely you can see the little girl with a barrette in her hair to the left of the Christmas tree, holding the dog and smiling. It still gives me chills! Neighborhood research revealed a little girl with a dog who'd lived down the street had passed. My boss suddenly became a believer.

I was now hosting house parties, doing readings, and appearing on local TV. I was starting to get known, and hotel guests began to recognize me and ask what I was doing there. I began to ask myself the same question. I was torn, but I also knew I couldn't hang on to both worlds. First I reduced my days working at the hotel to three, then two times a week. It wasn't easy to detach. I hated to leave the staff. They felt like family. I had moved up the ranks and now had the best shift and a job people stayed in for years. Seaport was voted one of Boston's best places to work, and I was up for supervisor.

I was still young and making more than an EMT working on an ambulance—enough to go out with friends and drive a nice car. For all practical purposes, I had it made.

WEIGHING MY OPTIONS

Before that psychic told me otherwise, being a paramedic was my dream job. They do much of the same work as a physician and I wanted to work in an emergency room. The idea of providing comfort and healing in a fast-paced environment was very appealing.

So I looked into becoming a paramedic. It's a very expensive process that requires a lot of school and study. The job was still very appealing, but my psychic gift was taking off and I was feeling pulled to see where it took me. It seemed I was at a crossroads. I was starting to do small group readings and felt people really needed me to heal their grief. I realized this was another way to help people heal and I wanted to see where this road would take me.

I remembered the psychic who told me I had a bigger purpose in life. Becoming a paramedic could wait. I decided to give mediumship my full attention and took a leave from work, which was a hard decision to make. I wasn't making more than ten or twenty dollars a reading—a little more for small groups—and spirit doesn't pay benefits! But once I made the decision, I felt like heaven opened its doors. My boss bent over backward to support me, really helping me make the leap. Everyone at work encouraged me to follow my path, and Seaport even held my job open for six months. Many of those amazing people are still my friends to this day.

A HEAVEN-SENT OPPORTUNITY!

Although I worried mediumship wouldn't pay the bills, things began to take off as soon as I took that leap of faith. Once I focused all my energy on this career path, I started to do bigger events. I had more time for private sessions. I got calls from radio bookers and publicists. I appeared on TV and local radio.

Invited to teach at the Learning Annex, I did a pay-per-view segment in New York City on tapping into your psychic ability, which helped me learn a few things myself. I already had experi-

say she was working on her trust issues. Her boyfriend had finally proposed but she wasn't sure he would really marry her. Despite all the evidence, she still didn't trust him.

Many clients want to know if someone is interested in them romantically. But it doesn't end there. Will the person want to be exclusive, move in together, get engaged, marry, or have kids together? The questions and the stress never stop. Watching how people deal with these issues has made me realize something that has helped me in my own relationship with Alexa. Don't race to reach the next milestone. Enjoy getting to know your special some-one and trust the relationship will unfold as it was meant to.

Spirit has provided me with a lot of insight, but I don't consider myself a spiritual teacher, per se. I just don't feel I fit that mold. When I think of a spiritual teacher, I think of an energy worker like Deborah King. At this moment that's just not me. I feel like I'm the student, learning a new language, happy to have the opportunity to learn from the living and those on the other side.

One thing my work has taught me is that all healing comes from within, and if you're diagnosed with an illness there is a mind/body/spirit connection. No matter what the emotional or physical problem, healing requires a positive mindset.

For example, one woman, desperate to talk to me after losing her mother, signed up for my cruise. She didn't book her flight in time. Airlines were sold out. The flights available would make the connection too tight so she decided to drive, fearing she would not have enough time to make it from the airport to the ship. She drove twenty-four hours, almost missing the ship! By the time she ran through the cruise terminal they'd already lifted the gangway. She was so distraught, the gatekeepers let her through. Maintenance heard her banging on the ship's door and let her in. She was the talk of the ship. Exhausted from the drive and the stress, she slept the first two days, barely leaving her room to eat in the dining room, where people could sense her desperation.

I went to see what I could do for the poor thing. She was a mess. Heartache showed in her face, posture, and attire. Her mother had been her best friend. When she passed, everything fell apart. Nobody in her family would talk to her because they were fighting over the estate. Her husband was divorcing her, and she'd developed fibromyalgia. Somehow she managed to get on the cruise ship to see me.

As soon as I was in the room, her mother came right through and told her to leave her room and enjoy the cruise. The woman dressed up and went to dinner. Everyone told her how beautiful she looked and made her feel welcome. By the next night she was disco dancing on deck. She ended up having a great cruise just by being open to her mother's advice from heaven. Last I heard she was back to work, repairing relations with her brother, and feeling healthier and happier.

Readings can only heal if you choose to open the door with the key spirit hands you.

SUGGESTED VIDEO: Google "Matt Fraser Psychic Medium on the Street" to watch as I deliver messages to random shoppers downtown.

TOOLS FOR LIFE

I started working at a very young age, often holding down more than one job at a time. My busy schedule never bothered me because there was something about each job that I found enjoyable and fulfilling. I worked with great people, and naturally sought out jobs where I had the opportunity to help others.

It is so important to pay attention to and appreciate the opportunities that come your way. Every day you come in contact with people who have the potential to enrich your life by providing support, friendship, or guidance. And wherever you go, you can look for ways to be kind and helpful to other people.

You have to be open to the signs the universe sends your way, even if what unfolds is not what you were expecting! When I was working toward my goal of becoming a paramedic, I wanted to help and heal people. Who would have guessed the turn that my career would take? But really, is being a medium so different from being a paramedic or EMT? After all, both work with people in pain and help them heal—it's just that paramedics heal the body, while a medium heals the soul.

There were many signs and synchronicities that came together to bring me to where I am today. You don't have to be a psychic to recognize them, just keep a watchful eye out for signs that the universe sends to you.

While you're waiting for guidance, be alert and thankful for the life you are living. If you are experiencing sorrow or loss, take time to focus on the positive memories and situations that gave you joy and happiness.

Joy attracts more joy—so even when life throws me a curve, I remind myself of everything I'm grateful for. That habit of gratitude lifts me up, and it can do the same for you. It is a habit that has helped me reach my goals, and it can help you reach yours.

Each night I think of the list of things I am grateful for, and then I pray.

You might want to write down what you are grateful for—it trains your mind to seek the positive and that affects your thinking. Feel the joyful energy in your heart and mind, and take it with you everywhere you go.

CHAPTER 5

"You're a Wizard, Harry!"

In earlier chapters I talked about seeing visions when I was very young and how my grandmother returned to be with me after she passed. I shared how Mom and Grandma did readings for friends and neighbors. You might ask why I needed a tearoom psychic to open my eyes to my own abilities. Why did my mediumship come as a surprise with so many signs and hints along the way? The explanation is simple. Despite my gifts, I was a typical kid, living my life. My grandma had her cards. Mom did readings for friends. I took it all for granted and didn't really pay attention.

It was the same with Dad. I never wondered why the navy took him all over the world, why he brought back presents from China, why he was gone so long, or what he was doing there. I was just happy to see him when he came home.

A GIFT FROM GRANDMA MARY

When I tried the white-light meditation the psychic recommended, too many messages came through to ignore my gift. I sat down at the kitchen table to tell Mom. It was like the scene in Harry Potter where Hagrid tells Harry he is a wizard. Mom finally described in detail the family gift, which she and Grandma had always known I had too. Then she ran upstairs. I could hear her rummaging in the attic. She came down holding a small bundle wrapped in fabric.

Grandma made these cards and asked me to give them to you when you're ready.

I unwrapped the package. I was surprised to find regular playing cards with markings on them, not a tarot deck. However, lots of psychics use regular playing cards that they learn to interpret. Their insights really come through the cards from spirit.

I started playing around with the cards and found they worked differently for me than for my mother. I didn't interpret messages from the cards at all. Instead, I'd lay them out and use them to open my mind and trigger visions the way coffee grinds and tea leaves did for my mother. I would focus on the cards and ask a question. The answer came through in my mind.

THE SECRET IS OUT

We didn't make an official announcement to friends and family, but you know how it is. Word gets out.

I was doing small events and radio interviews. Mom helped with events. She would post my appearances on Facebook, where friends and relatives would see her posts. We have a big family, and many started coming to my events. I was meeting some for the first time. A distant cousin came up to me at an event and said her father had gone to a family member who was a medium but never told her who it was. He had never revealed her identity but did say the psychic told him he had a heart condition and he would die at fifty-seven if he didn't see a doctor and make lifestyle changes. He never followed her advice, though he did go for several readings. He passed at fifty-seven of a heart attack. We put the pieces together and figured out it was Grandma.

DIGGING INTO MY GRANDMOTHER'S PAST

My cousin's story intrigued me. I wanted to learn more about my grandma's secret psychic gift. I found Grandma's address book, which contained names I recognized but hadn't heard mentioned in years. Mom told me which of them likely knew about Grandma's gift. Then I started calling. I said I was investigating Grandma's psychic ability, asked if they knew about her gift, and mentioned that I was a medium too. Most had already heard through the grapevine or Mom's Facebook posts that I was a medium who'd inherited my gift from Grandma.

Some who hadn't known she was a medium recalled how Grandma always seemed to know things about people—for instance, a family member who'd died of an unknown cause. Early one week Grandma got a call that her cousin had the flu; later that week she got a call saying this relative only had hours to live. No one was allowed to know what was going on—it was a big secret. No one could ask what happened, but Grandma had a feeling and told Mom the woman had died of cirrhosis of the liver. Grandma mentioned this feeling to family members but everyone said, *No, it wasn't that.* Years later my parents, who were researching family genealogy, came across this relative's death certificate. Sure enough, she'd died of cirrhosis of the liver. Grandma just knew things.

One of Grandma's best friends remembered the day her son fell down a department store escalator. He wasn't badly hurt but did hit his head. His mother spent the day at the hospital with him. When she got home she called Grandma, who immediately asked, *Who fell down the escalator?*

Grandma told people about her gift very selectively. She was only open with those she felt would be nonjudgmental. Like I said earlier, not even my grandfather knew that my grandmother was a medium. I would ask him all the time, "Poppy, do you remember Grandma giving readings?" He would say to me, "No. I worked three jobs! I never knew what your grandmother was doing. As long as she had dinner ready, that's all I cared about." Poppy said there were times, however, when he walked in and caught Grandma Mary at the kitchen table with women hovered around large, strange cards and the room dead silent. He would come in confused, saying, "What's happening here?" and my grandmother would cover by saying, "We are playing cards; go in the other room." She never told him what they were actually doing, and my grandfather never questioned it. I mean, who would actually think their wife was channeling the dead in the kitchen?

It's funny because Poppy truly never knew what it was that I even did! As my fame started to grow, my grandfather would ask me, "What is your job? What is it you do?" I used to say, "Poppy, I'm a MEDIUM like Grandma. I speak to the dead." My grandfather would say, "Ohhhh a medium; I understand." Next thing you knew, people would come up to him saying, "I want to see your grandson. I heard he is performing at Foxwoods Resort Casino." My grandfather would tell them, "Yes, you need to go! My grandson is amazing; he's fantastic; he's some type of a comedian!" When I brought my grandfather to my shows, he truly started to understand what I did. He started to put together the pieces of the story and all the clues that he missed showing his own wife was a psychic medium. Poppy learned to enjoy what I did and coming to my shows, so much so that he joined me on the road and came to all my events, working as my "hand stamper," although instead of stamping the guests hands, I would catch him holding the hands of the pretty women!

MOM'S STORY

While I was digging into Grandma's past, I bugged Mom with a million questions about how she started doing her own readings. The answer was surprising!

As a little girl, my mom attended psychic workshops with her mother. For fifty cents they joined a group of psychics and mediums in a Rhode Island tearoom. Everyone got a reading and did a psychic share. Grandma felt comfortable around these like-minded people; Mom, not so much. Grandma loved these workshops and gave her own readings after listening to the leader. Mom was uncomfortable sharing. The group's leader knew Mom was psychic and would ask what she could see when she did a tea-leaf reading. Mom was afraid. She'd lie and say she couldn't see anything.

At home Grandma would lay out her own cards or set up the tea leaves and ask Mom what she saw. Mom would say she didn't see anything. She was only seven or eight years old and afraid to be wrong, like when you're afraid to answer a parent who's helping with homework and tells you to *figure it out yourself. You know the answer.*

The workshop leader recognized Mom's talent and tried to work with her, but Mom was too young, nervous, and conflicted. She just wasn't ready.

ENCOUNTERING CHALLENGES ALONG THE WAY

Respect and credibility can be elusive to the young. One time I just could not get validated during a demonstration. Messages were coming in loud and clear, but some recipients kept saying *no, no, no.* Later the owner of the spiritual center came up to me as I was packing up. She knew most of the participants. Evidently my readings had all been spot-on, but my youth made them unwilling to open up and trust me. They often said things like, "How is this young kid psychic, he is barely even out of high school!" As if that makes a difference.

While researching my psychic relatives, I was also reading about other mediums and attending various readings. One medium encouraged me; a second said she didn't see it. *Don't quit your day job—this mediumship thing is not going to happen for you!* I was told.

I felt discouraged and confused until I realized how wrong she was! Doors were opening all over the place. My own psychic vision revealed she was coming from a place of insecurity and jealousy.

AN EARLY READING

One reading really stands out because of the many emotions it stirred up. I was only twenty at the time and still living at home. Dad had no idea what I could do.

Our neighbors across the street really wanted a baby. The doctors said the wife couldn't have a baby naturally so they tried everything, spending thousands on in vitro fertilization. They'd been so hopeful throughout the process, but one day Mom saw the wife crying as she got out of her car. She walked across the street to ask what was wrong. The neighbor said the IVF hadn't worked and, being in the military, she only had a short window to get pregnant. Mom felt so bad and wanted to help.

At the time I was working the night shift. I was still sleeping when Mom came into my room to wake me up and ask me to see if I could see anything that would help her neighbor. I knew about the woman's struggles with infertility and was able to quickly tune in. I told my mother she would have a baby without in vitro. I saw the baby waiting in heaven and knew she would be pregnant before long. Mom said I had to go tell her. We went together, me still groggy and in pajamas. I could see Mom's neighbor felt better as soon as I told her what I'd seen. We sat around talking until her husband, who was also in the military, walked in with tears in his eyes. His wife had called earlier with the disappointing news. He'd come home to comfort his wife, not entertain neighbors. She told him what I'd said, thinking it would comfort him. Instead he threw us out of the house. He said he was done. They'd already spent money on in vitro. It didn't work. He didn't need anyone giving his wife false hope. My heart sank. I was trying to do something good, but he didn't want to hear it. He had already come to terms with the fact that there would be no pregnancy and that was that. We left. I felt awful.

Several months later she ran across the street to tell us she was pregnant and they were naming the baby Matthew! Despite her husband's resistance, she'd accepted my reading. This helped take the pressure off. Nature did the rest and they now have two children.

I was very pleased to have reassured my neighbor she'd eventually become a mother. There were more proud moments of the kind to come. For instance, preparing to wrap up a demonstration, I became aware of a spirit waving me over to a young woman in the audience who turned out to be her granddaughter. The spirit told me her granddaughter had been going through fertility treatments and given birth to two girls. The husband didn't want his wife to try again after two miscarriages. He didn't want her to experience the pain of losing another child. They'd pretty much given up on their dream of having four children. I told her the news. "Your grandmother is telling me you will have one more; this time a boy."

"I can't believe you said that. I have one egg left that's frozen, and it's a boy."

I feel certain they now have three children and I would love to hear from them. When I read for someone in these situations, I ask them to let me know what happened. They usually do!

People want to tell you how things turned out. I love updates and am always getting invited to weddings, baby showers, and communions. I even get invited to funerals for people who knew they were dying and wanted to know what death and heaven were like.

At the same time some family members feel threatened and can get freaked out. When my dad's side of the family started finding out about my gift, they wanted to sit down with me and see what it was all about. I read for my dad's mother and uncle. Some things came up for my grandmother that she didn't think her grandson should know about, making the reading too uncomfortable to continue. One thing that came up was how she almost died giving birth to my dad.

My dad's uncle lives in Maine. Though a huge skeptic, he still wanted a reading but didn't want his wife to know, so we did the reading at a card table in his basement. He had no idea what to expect. He turned the lights off thinking that we needed to be in total darkness to channel a message from spirit. I laughed and explained to him that's not how it works. Spirit delivers messages to me at all hours and at any place or time as long as I am listening.

I began reading for him, and his close friend with cancer, whom he'd visited regularly, came through.

One night my great-uncle went to check on his friend, as he did many times during the week. There was a note posted on the front door that read: *Don't come in. Call 911.* But it was too dark out to read, so my great-uncle went inside to discover that his friend had shot himself.

The friend had a message for my great-uncle. *Please tell him I'm sorry he was the one who had to find my body. Tell him I'm not suffering anymore.*

During the reading, his friend explained in the reading that the pain was just too much for him and he didn't want to suffer anymore. He wanted my great-uncle to know that he left the note to save my great-uncle from finding him. Unfortunately, the note was never seen, and the memory of that moment was unforgettable. The reading had helped ease my great-uncle's grief. He was never a big believer in the afterlife, but this changed his mind.

SUGGESTED VIDEO: Google "Matt Fraser Eye Opening Psychic Reading For Sports Coach & Skeptic" to watch Coach Calhoun receive a reading for the first time ever.

TOOLS FOR LIFE

Do you ever wish you could talk to a friend or family member who has passed? It might not be possible to sit down and have coffee with them like you used to, but I can assure you that your loved ones are ALWAYS with you.

Keep an eye out for the signs your loved ones in heaven use to get your attention. These signs come in many different forms and often appear when you least expect them—but when you most need them. They are especially strong during special dates and times like birthdays and anniversaries.

You might be stressed, worried, or in need of reassurance, and then all of a sudden in the most random of places you'll find a penny from heaven—and you notice the date has a special significance.

Here are some simple ways you can invite more signs from heaven:

- Just ask. This is the first step to opening up your consciousness and allowing yourself to tap in and have proof of your loved ones' presence.

- Be direct. Send your loved one a message with your thoughts when need to hear from them and suggest a sign. "Mom, I miss you. Please send me a penny to let me know you're there."

- Listen to your intuition. Does that bird or butterfly give you a special feeling? Don't discount it. Your heart is recognizing a beautiful sign from a loved one.

• Don't overthink it. It's not an Easter egg hunt; just open your heart and allow the signs to come to you.

• Keep your loved one around with your words and thoughts. Doing this strengthens the connection and allows you to be more open to receiving signals from them.

Heaven has amazing ways of reaching you. The smallest of signs can communicate the biggest messages. So don't just pass them off as coincidence. The more open you are to signs, the more your loved ones will use them to communicate with you.

CHAPTER 6

Breaking the News to Dad

I inherited my spiritual gifts from Mom's side of the family. Grandma Mary and Mom didn't always broadcast their gifts—in those days people were not quite as accepting as they are now—but they had a way of making themselves known regardless.

Dad was another story. Born in Maine, he had had a strict Catholic upbringing. He was responsible, disciplined, and no-nonsense from a very young age. He joined the navy right after high school and spent twenty-one years serving his country, eventually reaching the rank of commanding officer. The navy strengthened his faith. He told me the Bible and a strong belief in God kept him going through some rough times.

A TWIST OF FATE

Fate brought my parents together. My dad was stationed in Rhode Island with a group of sailors. They had some free time one evening, so a group decided to go out on the town. They'd heard of this really great Providence nightclub but got lost. Remember, these were pre-GPS days. The clock was ticking on their window for a good time and they were wasting valuable time driving around. Finally they stopped at a gas station. It turned out the club they wanted was miles away, but there was another club just around the corner. They piled back in the car and headed to Sha-na-na's, a local nightclub where my mom and her friends hung out.

At the time Mom was a professional disco dancer who competed around town. She was on the dance floor with friends when Dad asked her to dance and was immediately smitten. He had only an hour or so before he had to get back to barracks or be declared AWOL. Mom wasn't about to give her phone number to a sailor she'd known for mere minutes, but she thought he was cute and told him she went there every Saturday to dance. He came back to see her the very next week and the rest is history. I'm convinced destiny brought them together!

Dad knew about the family gift when he married Mom. Let's just say he wasn't thrilled. Mediumship wasn't a big part of our day-to-day lives, but Grandma did get everyone to play psychic games when I was young, especially on long car rides. She'd sit in the front seat and take a card from a deck and say, "I'm going to psychically broadcast this card to you." We would have to guess the card. Dad went along out of respect, but after Grandma died he asked Mom to get rid of her tarot cards so their children wouldn't be influenced by "magic." Mom hid the cards in the basement and only took them out when Dad wasn't around. Dad was at the opposite extreme of the paranormal spectrum, so to speak. He didn't even approve of Halloween, though he tried not to be heavy-handed about it. He would bribe my sister and me with candy to encourage us to stay home, but after we ate the candy, we'd dress up and go trick or treating regardless.

Dad was still in the navy when my parents married. Mom traveled with him before I was born. Later we traveled together as a family until my sister came along. Maria is six years younger and definitely not a medium. She inherited Dad's skepticism and temperament. After Maria was born, we put down roots in Rhode Island. Dad felt very distant when he was at sea in these pre-texting, pre-Facetime, pre-Skype days when communication was limited to letters and the occasional email.

MOM CAN'T DENY HER GIFT

While Dad was gone, Mom would host gatherings for friends at the house. There was wine and pizza. Mom would take out her cards; her friends loved her readings! She would lay out her cards and make forecasts while a friend took notes.

One time the street had a garage sale. The neighbors put things out to sell. Having moved so much, we were used to traveling light, so didn't have much to sell. Garage sales were big on our street and this one went on for three consecutive weekends. Everyone looked forward to the sales, which were a fun way to socialize, make a few dollars, and clear out clutter.

Everyone on the block was hanging out on their front lawns having a good time, but just before lunchtime it got quiet. Mom was doing a card reading for a neighbor to pass the time, when a woman walked up and asked what was going on. Mom said she was doing a psychic reading. That was all she needed to hear! The woman begged for a reading. The next week Mom put a table out with a sign that read PSYCHIC READINGS $10. People loved it and lined up every Saturday. Mom thought there was no harm in it—the garage sales would be over at the end of the month. But she was wrong. It was no secret where she lived—she did the readings on our front lawn—so people kept knocking on our front door even after the garage sales ended. Mom started to panic at what Dad would say when he discovered the psychic tearoom in our living room! She told people to stop knocking on the door.

Mom was really conflicted. She loved Dad and didn't want to upset him, but a part of her couldn't deny her gift. She would say, "This is the last time I'm doing a reading," but it didn't take much to persuade her to pull her cards out *just this once*. She never wanted to hide what she was doing from Dad, but felt she had to share messages coming to her from spirit.

WE CAN'T HIDE THIS "PUPPY" FROM DAD ANY LONGER!

So it was no secret I couldn't tell my father I was following in Mom's footsteps. Dad never stopped me from seeing psychics and mediums. He was actually curious and would ask questions about my readings. I'd tell him what they said or that Grandma had come through, but I avoided saying I was told I was a medium too.

Things went along pretty quietly for a while, with Dad blissfully unaware his son was a practicing medium. My practice was slowly ramping up and finally began taking off. As fire commissioner, Dad was a public figure. People knew him. Once I did some radio spots, I knew my secret would be out. It was stressful keeping it from him. It felt like a sitcom where the kids bring home a puppy and try to hide it from their parents.

One night the deception got to be too much for Mom. She came in and sat on my bed. "This has gone too far; you have to tell your father."

I kept my eyes on my computer screen and tried to change the subject. I didn't want to have this conversation now or ever. Finally she sighed. "Okay, I'll tell him."

I was on eggshells for the next hour. Then I looked up to see Mom standing in the doorway with Dad. Normally a man of few words, he was even quieter than usual. We'd hid my work too well. Mom had hit Dad with a bombshell. He tried to be supportive and show pride in my initiative, but he said he didn't think this was the right business for me. Although I was saddened at his disapproval, I was relieved everything was finally out in the open. Surprisingly, Dad didn't freak out. He said he hoped I was just going through a phase and that I'd soon refocus my entrepreneurial talents on a very different business.

DAD HAS MY BACK!

People started realizing who I was and giving Dad positive feedback. People he respected would tell him how much I'd helped them. Our extended family became more aware of what was going on. We were surprised to learn someone on my dad's side of the family had been a medium. Dad's perspective changed. He was always an analytical kind of guy, so he started researching mediumship. The more he learned the more his mind opened to the whole idea. What he'd always considered unusual started to feel more mainstream and less threatening. He realized many people he knew got regular readings just like they went to a hairdresser or chiropractor.

Dad still isn't totally comfortable with mediumship. He does come to my events when he can but he generally sits outside. He likes to support me by offering advice regarding business and investments. We don't always see eye-to-eye—he's very conservative while I'm more creative—but I appreciate his perspective.

WARMING UP TO HIS SON'S NEW CAREER

People ask if I use my gift for my own benefit. I can't imagine not using it since it's such a major part of who I am. In business and every aspect of life, I rely heavily on intuition. It's like my superpower. I built my business with it. If I feel something is right, I go with it. I trust my intuition 100 percent. It hasn't let me down yet.

As much as he may try to put blinders on, Dad can't help becoming more accepting the more he's exposed to my work, and one reading in particular really made an impact. Dad agreed to help shoot B-roll video for an ad, which meant he would actually have to watch me work by positioning himself directly behind me as I did reading after reading. He couldn't escape to the lobby like he usually did. He just had to relax and try to enjoy it!

One reading that night affected him a lot. A young guy, who was hoping to connect with his grandfather, had brought his girlfriend with him. This was a bit unusual—women usually buy the tickets and drag the men along. I connected with his grandfather immediately and kept seeing professional sports. His grandfather mentioned the guy had his ring. Dad was amazed when the boy pulled his grandfather's ring—a player's ring—out of his pocket. It turned out the grandfather had played for the NHL. This was concrete proof Dad could see and touch. It was a very positive, loving connection. Dad just loved it! It was a very heartwarming reading with a grandfather happy to see his grandson following in his footsteps and playing hockey, too.

Unlike the rest of our family, Dad's not a big talker. He prides himself on being a man of few words, and I naturally assumed he doesn't talk about what I do to friends and associates. But it appears that's not always the case. Once, on a consulting assignment in Pennsylvania, he got to talking with a man he was working with and it came up in conversation that I was a medium. The guy was pretty skeptical, but Dad really convinced the guy and offered him tickets to one of my events. The man came to my show and was very impressed. I was even more impressed and surprised Dad had been such an advocate of my work—that was really cool.

PROTECTION FROM THE SPIRIT REALM

People often ask if I get messages for myself. Spirit doesn't send me lottery numbers, but I do remember one time when I was certain someone was looking out for me and my dad. At the time I was still an EMT. The Seaport Center asked me to work a Boston Marathon detail. I was looking forward to going—working an event like that would have been like a fun field trip.

Normally I never missed work no matter what, but the day before the race I had a sick feeling in my stomach. I was feeling physically ill and also getting messages not to go that I couldn't ignore. In a very much out-of-character move, I called my boss to cancel. As fire commissioner, Dad naturally had to attend the marathon but began getting a terrible headache as the event got underway. That was unusual—Dad didn't get headaches. Finally, with the race almost over, he decided to leave early and was heading home when he got word of the Boston Marathon bombing. He turned the car around and returned to help get people to safety. I heard the news too, and was getting in the car to rush down to help when Dad called to say there was no need because there were enough volunteers. I also remember calling my father to tell him there was another bomb. I was really nervous about it and told him to be careful. I know this incident convinced my father that my ability could be used for good. We never talked to each other about the synchronicity that kept us both safe. I could swear Dad asked if I had other details about the second bomb, but I found it strange that I was clearly not supposed to be there.

Spirit protected us both that day, and Dad's come a long way from begging Mom to discard her tarot cards. Now he's gaining new perspective on how mediumship can help and heal, and he assists at my events.

After Dad opened his heart and mind to the path I'd chosen, he found that many people he knew were already a part of this world.

SUGGESTED VIDEO: Google "Psychic Matt Fraser— Medium with a Message Video" to watch my second live group reading video that my dad helped out with.

TOOLS FOR LIFE

Although mediumship runs in the family on my mother's side, the ability to connect with spirit isn't something everyone can accept. You've probably heard the advice—especially around the holidays—that you should avoid discussing sex, politics, and religion. It might seem like talking to dead people should be somewhere on that list! But avoiding controversial topics isn't necessary as long as they are discussed with love and mutual respect.

Members of my extended family are all passionately different—which makes for lively conversations at family meals and holidays. But it all works out just fine because we deeply respect one another's viewpoints even when we see things differently.

Here are some things to keep in mind when you know you'll be coming into contact with someone who has different opinions about one of the "hot topics."

- Look for common ground. I can't tell you how many times someone has told me that they are uncomfortable with the idea of mediumship because of their religion. But when I ask if they ever feel like a loved one is watching over them, or if they have conversations in their head with someone who has passed, the answer is usually yes. Having that discussion helps them to realize that we're not so far apart!

- Don't fixate on the sensitive topic. Now that I've come clean with my dad, and most of the people I know are very aware of what I do, I don't avoid the topic of medi-umship. But that's just one thing about me—I also love to talk about movies, travel, fashion, pets—you name it!

- Have a sense of humor and do your best not to take what people say too personally. You may take very different paths in life, but the cornerstone to maintaining strong family ties will be appreciation, respect, and acceptance. That and love can be the glue that holds the family bonds together.

CHAPTER 7

Skeptics, Nonbelievers, and Negative Nancys

love connecting people with their loved ones in heaven. The reactions I get are overwhelmingly supportive and positive, but I've also encountered some who are skeptics, at least at first!

SHOCKING THE SHOCK JOCKS

I remember an invitation from the hosts of a popular morning drive-time show from Boston. I had already done a few appearances, but not yet before such a large audience. I was very excited. If I'd been a little more experienced, I might have known to do my due diligence. Instead I got a funny feeling listening to the show on my way to the radio station. The DJs were making sarcastic comments about interviewing a medium later that morning. As it turns out, they were *shock jocks* who'd invited me so they could mock and discredit me. During more than an hour in the greenroom, I had time to get more nervous with every passing minute.

A porn star was on the schedule just ahead of me and I realized I was in over my head. This kind of show was new to me. What the heck was going on? I called my publicist. *Why did you book me on this show?* She encouraged me to go on and just do my thing. *Be yourself.* I was very nervous but had a feeling that it would turn out okay.

I finally got called into the studio. The hosts started out being sarcastic, evidently gearing up to make me look like a fool and a fake.

Surprisingly it didn't turn out that way. The hosts' skepticism began to fade once the phones lit up. They stopped joking around as I started taking calls.

The first caller was a girl. I said her deceased father was coming through and was holding a cat.

A cat? The girl seemed confused, and the DJs snickered, ready to pounce.

"It's a big gray cat named Smoky."

The girl started crying. "Smoky was my cat when I was a little girl!"

The hosts stopped laughing.

I was originally scheduled for ten minutes—plenty of time to make me look like a fool. I ended up staying for the rest of the show. More and more calls came through and there were some great connections. I love taking radio calls—no distractions from the audience. It's easier to focus on what the spirits are saying.

The shock jocks invited me back the next week, then wrote me in as a regular. That risky radio show turned into the best thing I could have done. I was reaching a new audience, who didn't believe in psychics, with messages of healing and changing their way of thinking.

These DJs were pretty funny and really liked to mess around with me. They'd lost their skepticism but still enjoyed teasing me about my conversations with the dead. On-air they still gave me a hard time. Off-air they'd be like, *Hey, Matt, my grandma just passed. I was wondering . . .*

WHO IS PAUL?

There have been times my readings were so accurate people accused me of paying callers to make me look good on-air. I couldn't do that if I wanted to—it's really hard to get through to a popular drive-time radio station. A few times people called in just to deny everything I said and trip me up.

One day a friend of the hosts showed up with coffee for everyone while we were still on-air. The hosts couldn't resist the opportunity to test my mediumship.

"Hey, Matt, see if you can read George!"

They asked George to step in front of the microphone. I saw his mother behind him, who said some nice things to her son then added one more thing. "Please tell Paul thank you for taking care of me."

George looked at me. "There's no Paul. No one named Paul helped Mom."

The response was crazy. People were saying here was proof I was nothing but a fake. They said I'd flubbed the reading. Then while on-air, something astonishing happened. George's cell phone rang. It was Paul. He was furious. George had forgotten about his mother's good friend who'd been with her through her entire illness. I don't know if George was trying to make me look bad or if he'd blocked the sad memories around his mother's death, but Paul sure gave him an earful. He came back on-air to apologize.

Being a regular on the radio show gave me a whole new audience—a macho, rock-and-roll crowd who loved their trucks . . . as you might imagine, not my usual demographic! It was fun to see all these tatted-up men in leather jackets showing up at events after hearing me on-air. These guys would come in looking all tough and intimidating until their mothers came through. Then they'd start crying. There are no tough guys when it comes to love and family! Everyone feels the same love once we let ourselves open up.

BEWARE OF UNWELCOME GIFTS

Often people who get closure and healing from a great reading can't wait to share that experience with a loved one, so they gift private readings to someone they think will benefit, too. These gifts are generally well received, but sometimes it's not the right time for a reading. The gift giver doesn't realize the recipient may not be ready. They just assume it's the right thing to do because they had such a great experience.

A man called to book a reading for his wife. He hoped his father-in-law would come through. When my booker (my mom!) called the wife to reschedule, she said she wanted to cancel. She didn't want a reading but her husband insisted. Mom suggested a new date, which just so happened to be the anniversary of her father's death! The wife was pretty quiet. Her husband said it was a sign and encouraged her to move forward with the reading.

We didn't know what was going on behind the scenes when she Skyped in for the reading. I realized right away her father had passed.

I was getting great details—all kinds of stuff about how she'd grown up in a three-decker multifamily home. Different relatives lived on each floor. I was getting messages about how guilty she felt for not going to see her father when he was ill. All she did was call. I knew she felt bad she wasn't there when he died.

She kind of confirmed what I was saying, nodding a bit, but she was still acting a bit weird. I could tell she wasn't really paying attention. I could see her looking around the room. I was worried there was a technical issue. Maybe she couldn't really hear me. I asked if we had a bad connection.

No, I can hear you. I just don't believe in the afterlife or that souls can communicate. You are getting things right, but I don't want to do this.

I was frustrated and asked if there was anything I could do for her. Not only was I trying to get through to her, her father was trying too, and sending me all kinds of information. It all started with a giant sign from spirit when we rescheduled her reading on his birthday.

I'm going to end the call. Please don't tell my husband. Let's just stop the reading now.

She told me she'd only agreed to do the reading to make her husband happy, but she wasn't into it.

After she ended our Skype connection I did something I don't normally do. I really needed to know what had gone wrong, so I contacted her father on the other side. He explained that his daughter was going through a divorce. His son-in-law had gifted the reading because he believed her guilt about her father was among the reasons she was divorcing him. She'd been bringing her sadness about her father's death into the marriage. The husband hoped his father-in-law would reach out from heaven and help her heal, and at the same time put in a good word for him. The father said his daughter had always been stubborn. She felt her husband was trying to manipulate her by trying to involve his spirit. I never learned how he and his wife fared. I will always wonder if they were able to heal their relationship another way.

This reading and similar ones taught me that some people are not ready. Some fear mediumship itself; others spirits from the other side. I usually don't meet them unless they're dragged to an event!

"I CAN'T (OR I WON'T) HEAR YOU!"

People are resistant to readings for all kinds of reasons. Once I encountered an unexpected reaction during my very first reading of the night at a Newport, Rhode Island, event.

A man came through and said I had to speak with his wife, who was in the audience. I could feel he'd caused his own passing. He was so persistent that I walked over and told her I had a message from her husband.

I have no husband who passed.

A man is here who says he was your husband and shot himself in the head. He apologized for having so much anger that got in the way of your relationship.

That's not my husband. I have no husband. That's my ex.

He said his name was Steven.

That was my ex's name.

When Spirit comes through, they don't tell me "I'm the ex-husband, half-brother in law, cousin that was three times removed from the family, et cetera. Many times, stepfathers will come through as fathers, half-brothers will come through as brothers and sometimes even ex-husbands will come through as husbands. In heaven they do not check for marriage certificates. Connections are determined by the bond and relationship you share with a special person. She was determined to reject my reading, even though she reluctantly confirmed the names I was getting. It soon became obvious she didn't like her ex and didn't want to hear from him. The audience was on the edge of their seats. They couldn't believe I'd gotten so many details correct, yet she still wasn't denying the messages. As she was leaving, she looked at me and said, "That wasn't my ex-husband." She couldn't resist having the last word!

Why would a person like this attend an event, then not accept an accurate reading? In this case, the woman didn't want a reading from her ex. She was closed off to him even after he passed. It's like refusing to answer the phone when your ex's number pops up or blocking someone on Facebook. Some people just don't want to hear from a particular person. I never found out who she *did* want to hear from.

LOOKING FOR THE "TELL"

People who don't want to believe I'm connecting to spirit always have something to say, even if the readings are on target and everyone else is crying.

If a reading is too vague, they call that a *cold reading*, where a medium says general things that could apply to anyone. But mediumship is not black and white, and some messages are more detailed than others. It depends on the soul doing the communicating and a million other factors. Sometimes I can't catch the message because the impressions are coming through so fast. If I give too many details and they're all correct, people accuse me of doing research beforehand. I have no idea who will turn up at an event, and audience members don't wear name tags to identify them. Even if I could somehow find a way to find this type of personal info about audiences ahead of time, where would I find the time unless I were a Facebook algorithm?!

Others accuse me of paying people to pack my events. I often do more than twenty readings a night with audiences of up to five hundred people. Where would I find the money?

I understand people have questions. I find it amusing that some people look at it like a magic trick and just try to figure out my method. I prefer skeptics who remain open to being convinced once they see the evidence. I think we should all be open to changing our minds when presented with new information about anything in life.

Real nonbelievers can't be convinced. They've already made up their mind. It's like someone who goes to the doctor and is told,

You have a heart condition and have to change your diet, lose weight, and come back to see me in three months. They refuse to take the doctor's advice even after they see the EKG results. Even if they have a heart attack, they'll blame it on something else.

I try not to let negative people upset me. They're usually negative for a reason, often something they can't get past that's clouding their vision like foggy glasses they can't wipe clean. People who can't see clearly keep stumbling into the same bad situations. They're unable to open their minds. A soul who loves them may try to send a message. This can be an opportunity to learn a lesson from the past and not repeat the same mistake over and over.

I AM A ROCK

Some people like to be impenetrable and pride themselves on being unreadable. I met a woman once who was going to do some work for me and wasn't looking for a reading. In fact, when I told her I was a medium she insisted *no one can ever read me.* As she was telling me this, her brother came through really strong from the other side. I tried to tell her, but she kept talking and wouldn't receive the message. I felt bad. Her brother really wanted to talk to her.

Some people want to test me. One woman called up desperate to hear from her mother on the other side.

I need to talk to my mom. I need to talk to my mom.

I was trying to connect with her mother, but she wouldn't listen to a word I was saying. The energy wasn't good and I wound up shutting the call down. She must have called twelve times wanting another reading. I finally agreed to a Skype call. Her mother came through and told me she was struck and killed by a car while walking with her family. I could clearly see everyone standing around after the accident. The family was crying. Her mother told me her daughter had brought a blanket. I was conveying all this to my client when suddenly she stood up and crossed her arms. She glossed over the info I'd gotten right. She was set on asking a question I couldn't answer.

What day was the accident?

I could see a sixteen, but there was no point. She didn't want to hear a message from her mother; she just wanted to test me. Readings are not designed to share details; they're designed to share a message. That's what matters. Souls come through with important messages they need to share, messages that are precious to the people who receive them with an open heart.

People come to readings with different motives. I remember a woman's fiancé coming through during a phone reading to tell me how upset he was that they hadn't married. He'd committed suicide and wanted to tell her why. She was quiet. I kept asking if she was there.

How do I know that's really him? What did he wear? What nickname did he call me?

Something felt off and I told my mom I didn't feel comfortable moving forward with the session. When Mom called, the woman said that she was also a medium and she wasn't interested in a reading. She was just trying to get info to help her own business!

I TELL PEOPLE I'M A "FORESIGHT CONSULTANT," NOT A MEDIUM

Sometimes people's pain won't allow them to accept the answer from spirit. Losing a loved one to suicide or overdose is hard to accept. Families might prefer to think they died of foul play. It's usually the obvious scenario, but not always.

I've found the people I encounter in my work and personal life generally fall into one of a few categories. Half are receptive, while 20 percent or so are totally unreceptive and don't believe in mediums at all. The other 30 percent are conflicted; one part of them believes, another part prevents them from being totally open, perhaps due to their religious beliefs or an insistence on disbelieving anything that cannot be scientifically proven.

When I was visiting my grandfather in the nursing home, people started recognizing me. A resident came up to me to ask why others were coming up to me. I told her I was a medium. She said, *I'm sorry, my church won't let me talk about that.*

I used to try to change people's minds until I realized that's not why I'm here. I don't want to waste my energy passing people's tests. I can't even explain how I do what I do. How can I convince someone else?

My gift is right here for people to see for themselves. I'm not here to validate mediumship, per se. I'm here to deliver messages. Mom convinced me of our sacred duty to pass on messages. I like to take it one message at a time and keep it between myself, the soul, and my client. That's all the proof most people need. I remember being at Foxwoods Resort Casino for my first casino show. A security guard was assigned to escort me to the event room. The security guard never left me as I changed into event attire. He was a nice guy and stayed very close, which I found a bit odd—I'm not the president! After the event he came up to me.

I don't believe in this stuff. I was determined to learn your secret. I kept my eyes on your mother to catch her signaling you. I looked for wires and headpieces but didn't see a thing. You're the real thing!

This guy wasn't staying so close to be my bodyguard. He was checking me out for wires! We later became friends and I did many more events at Foxwoods. He always requested to be assigned to me and encouraged his coworkers to check out my show.

People who know me are pretty accepting of what I do. They've seen my events, and even if they were undecided or skeptical at first, they usually leave feeling they've learned something. People will always believe what they want to believe. In the end you need to focus on those you can heal. There are so many!

CROSSED WIRES . . .

Sometimes people call in to set up one reading for multiple people. We tell them calls are one-on-one. Nevertheless, another person will get on the call anyway, which can get confusing because I pick up on the energy of the person listening in. Often people just don't listen, even though Mom explains this policy whenever she books a reading.

One time a woman was on the line for a reading. I started with a prayer. I could tell her husband had passed, but she said no. I said her husband's name was Harry. Then more people came through. Suddenly she put me on hold. When she came back she said, *I'm sorry. Harry was my friend's husband. She's been listening in. Why is this happening during my reading?*

That's why we ask you not to have people on the line with you.

But I paid for the reading!

She didn't understand that payment was immaterial to spirit, who is not concerned with invoices.

THAT'S NOT MY READING!

A grandmother came through at an event. Two sisters in front stepped forward—one cried, the other stood with her arms crossed. Grandma kept saying how grateful she was her granddaughters had taken her off life support. The stoic sister kept pointing to her sibling. Every time I asked for confirmation, she just pointed to her sister. *That's my sister.*

I had no idea what she meant. Then she explained: *I didn't want this reading.* She'd decided this was her sister's reading. Grandma was coming through for both granddaughters, but this woman wanted her own private reading, without her sister present, and wasn't going to listen to anything I said!

Sometimes privacy is an issue. One time while giving a reading on-air during a morning talk show, a baby was coming through, which the mother denied. I realized she had terminated the pregnancy and preferred not to talk about it publicly. Other times I get the feeling the person doesn't want to hear a message in front of a parent or spouse. There are some things people just don't want said out loud.

A woman came to my event whose daughter had died from a drug overdose. I got that the daughter was brilliant but became addicted to pills in med school and began stealing pills from patients as a resident. She went into cardiac arrest. The parents didn't know for sure about the drugs but they had their suspicions, and everything came out at this event. The mother was embarrassed that the audience would think of her daughter as a drug addict. The rest of the family looked at me in shock. They wouldn't confirm anything. The mother booked a private reading later and received an amazing healing message from her daughter.

SUGGESTED VIDEO: Google "Matt Fraser From Skeptic to Believer Video" to watch two skeptics receive a reading on live television. You will not believe their reactions. This has got to be my all-time favorite video. I am happy to share it with you .

TOOLS FOR LIFE

When you attend a live event—a concert, a play, or an art exhibit—there's usually lots of anticipation beforehand. You look forward to what you'll see and hear, and might do something special to get the most out of it. Maybe you plan a wonderful meal or listen to the music from the play you're going to see. Being in the right mindset enhances your experience. It's the same with attending a mediumship demonstration.

Before attending a mediumship event, consider these tips:

1. Have an open heart and mind.

As you drive to a mediumship demonstration, you'll probably put your wishes out into the universe: "I hope I get a message from Dad!" That's perfectly fine, but try to be flexible and avoid locking in on one result. Maybe someone totally unexpected will come through, so trust that what is meant to be will be.

2. Look forward to learning from other people's readings.

I can't tell you how many times a reading applies to more than one person in the room. Spirit works in mysterious ways, so don't tune out if the medium is addressing someone else. There may be a lesson in it for you!

3. It's not over when the demonstration ends.

Being in the presence of a medium brings souls in heaven closer to you, even if you don't get a reading. Often, people leave my events and start noticing signs over the next few days that their loved ones are near.

4. Most important of all is to approach the event with a joyful heart.

Try letting go of grief and sadness and celebrating the love and sweet memories—these deep emotions will link you to those you love who have departed, and attract them to you.

I hope to see you at an event soon—I can assure you that even though not every single person will receive a reading, everyone in the room will leave feeling comforted by the loving presence of spirit.

CHAPTER 8

Ouija Boards, Psychic Protection, Positivity, and Hope

When I was young, souls often showed up uninvited to scare the heck out of me! Once I accepted my gift as I got older, the voices got softer and less insistent because I was listening to them. They were screaming to be heard, not to frighten me. I was able to talk about what I was experiencing with Mom, who had lots of wisdom from her mother to share, as well as things she'd experienced firsthand.

Mom always says dead people can't hurt you. It's the living you need to be afraid of. I now know that's true. However, I understand how people get nightmares about souls reaching out to connect with the living. People ask if my work opens a portal that evil spirits can pass through. It doesn't. Most spirits mean no harm and you can easily avoid the bad ones.

GHOSTS ARE OFTEN MISUNDERSTOOD

Mediumship couldn't be further removed from ghost stories and scary movies. Horror movies may be harmless fun—enjoying a good scare won't invite evil into your life—but they paint an inaccurate picture of the spirit realm. Intention matters a lot, and people generally don't go to scary movies to manifest ghosts and monsters into their everyday life. Those movies won't hurt you.

That being said, I don't spend a lot of time dwelling on negative spirits and I certainly don't go looking for trouble. I'd never dream of touching a *Ouija* board and I don't seek out haunted places. On the rare occasions where I've found myself in a haunted place, the spirits have behaved themselves. Not a one has ever kicked me or thrown me down the stairs.

Have I ever sensed a malignant spirit? Yes, but it's extremely rare. For every one even slightly negative soul, I've had a hundred connections with loving, well-meaning souls. You can avoid negative encounters by remembering that negative souls avoid groups. Energy displaces energy. A group will have too much positive energy to allow negative energy to come through. So you won't run into a negative spirit at the mall, casino, or mediumship event!

Displaced souls prefer empty places, abandoned houses, vacant businesses—anywhere energy is stagnant. Interestingly enough, they're not particularly drawn to graveyards, perhaps because all the love from both sides of the veil keeps them out.

Watch your intentions, keep your energy light, and play it safe. Don't mess around with spells, the occult, or *Ouija* boards!

SPOOKED IN NEWPORT

Sometimes what feels like a haunting or a malignant spirit is just an energy impression. Let me give you an example. I have a friend who owns a beautiful old mansion in Newport that was built in 1880. The family bought it strictly for entertaining and only visited to host big parties. For years they never stayed overnight, but eventually they decided to spend more time there.

Every time my friend slept there she felt uncomfortable. She could sense eyes watching her, and heaviness in the atmosphere. It was very unusual for her to feel this way—she's not superstitious or particularly intuitive.

The family was in the process of updating the house and had just finished installing a new electrical system. One day she decided to stay overnight to let contractors in the next morning to do some cabinetwork. As she was getting ready for bed all the lights went off by themselves. She checked the circuit breakers, but everything looked normal. She went around the house and turned all the lights back on. When she finished, they all went off again. She figured there must be a glitch in the new electrical system, but what could she do? She decided to go to sleep and deal with it in the morning, but she couldn't get comfortable. She had an uneasy feeling she couldn't explain. Suddenly the TV went on, then her cell phone started pinging. There were three dots from an unfamiliar number. Someone was trying to text her, but no message materialized. She was spooked! After tossing and turning she checked the alarm clock, which read four a.m. She gave up and went downstairs to await the contractors. Everything behaved quite normally while the workmen were in the house.

She called to tell me what happened. I agreed to visit her in a few weeks. When I got there, I immediately sensed the presence of spirit and a great sadness. It was more an energy impression than a haunting. I could feel one child had died here; other family members had fallen ill. I saw the family had called in a doctor back in the day, but without modern medicine they couldn't understand the illness and thought it was coming from the house itself.

When I walked in, I too felt the same emptiness, coldness, and stagnant energy my friend sensed. Although now beautifully restored with splendid fireplaces and carpets, the house felt as cold and sterile as a hospital. It was like walking into a museum, not a house.

I explained the idea of replacing leftover sadness with new energy. The house, which was boarded up between events, needed my friend's energy. There wasn't even a picture on the wall of the new owners. I told her the house needed her family's happy, loving presence, not just the occasional catered event. It needed its windows opened. It needed fresh air and an infusion of positive energy to counteract its negative history.

My friend started to visit more often, sometimes to enjoy a glass of wine with a friend. She even brought her pets with her. Soon the new life force edged the old negative energy out. The more positive energy that she brought into the house, the more she could feel the old energy leaving and the more she felt her house becoming a home.

THERE'S A LADY IN THESE SHEETS!

We are all energy. The things we touch often retain traces of this energy without being haunted. That's why psychics can pick up on your imprint from an old piece of clothing.

One day I went to my jewelry factory to check out some new designs for my line. After the meeting I went out to my convertible. The interior was soaked; I'd left the top open. My meeting went on longer than I'd anticipated and there'd been an unexpected downpour that we'd been too busy to notice. Linda, my jewelry designer, offered a box of rags to dry up the mess. I tried to soak up what I could, but I was distracted by a strange vision. There was an old woman who appeared to me while I was touching the rags.

I asked Linda where she'd gotten the rags. She said a rag service provided her with boxes of clean, recycled rags the factory used to clean and polish the jewelry. Suddenly I realized these were hospital sheets; the woman I was sensing had died on them. They weren't haunted; they just had energy clinging to them like pet hair to a couch. As I infused the rags with my own energy, my sense of the old woman gradually faded.

I can see how people might get freaked out at reusing sheets someone had died in, but there was nothing to be afraid of. The woman wasn't in the sheets. Her spirit had crossed over, leaving a trace of energy behind.

CROSSING OVER

Hauntings are rare. Souls usually cross right over without incident. Mediums don't help people cross over. They help replace old energy like I did in that Newport house. Transitioning the living to heaven is God's work, not mine.

Souls must be light to cross over, and usually are. Most people try to let go of old pain, trauma, regrets, and resentments before they die. Priests, rabbis, and others who minister to the soul can help. We have to forgive and be forgiven, and let go to get to the other side. However, a small percentage of souls are just too evil and too heavy to cross over. They get stuck, and that's how "dark spirits" exist. The truth is that it's so rare, you will most likely never run into one. The only people who are affected or come into contact with them are ghost hunters or people who delve into things they shouldn't. If you follow Mom's rule and don't go looking for trouble, you will be fine.

PROTECTION RITUALS

Dark spirits really can't hurt you when your own energy is positive, but here are a few things you can do to further protect yourself.

Remember how Mom said the only people you need to fear are the living? These techniques can help with earthly encounters, too.

• Imagine a mirrored wall around you reflecting negative energy away from you.

- Get to know your angels and guides; call upon them to protect you when needed.

- Burn sage to clear stagnant energy out of living spaces that feel uncomfortable.

- Infuse new spaces with your own energy. For instance, I personalize hotel rooms with photos of Alexa and our two cats. I also play some of my favorite disco tunes and open the window (if they open!) to let fresh air in.

Being a medium might seem like a morbid way to make a living, but I don't see it that way at all. On the contrary, I feel blessed to be able to spread light and help the living heal by letting them know their loved ones in heaven are still with them and wishing them the best!

SUGGESTED VIDEO: Google "Matt Fraser Healing, Love and Forgiveness" to discover the importance of letting go and learning to forgive.

DAD IN UNIFORM: After I was born, my dad, Rod, was off to sea in the navy for long periods of time. He was a commander at the time. I didn't get to see him much, and I really missed him as a child. It taught me to treasure the moments we get to spend with our friends and family.

MOM AND ME: My mom, Angela, and me at Foxwoods Resort Casino when I was three years old. Looking at this photo now, it's hard to believe that I am a resident performer there! You never know where life will take you.

FIRST FAMILY PHOTO: My psychic grandma, Mary, insisted we take this picture. Now I am so thankful because it was our last picture together before she passed away. While my dad, Rod, was out to sea, I was raised by my mom, Angela; my grandmother Mary; and grandfather Lou, all pictured. This is a photo I will always treasure.

OPERATOR IN HEAVEN: This picture makes me laugh, because it looks like I was doing phone readings at a young age! Actually, I have loved being on the phone since I was young. Now I feel like I run the phone lines in heaven.

NAVY BALL: My mom, Angela, and my dad, Rod, getting ready for the Navy Ball. I used to love to watch my dad get dressed up in his uniform. Seeing him court my mom taught me how to be a gentleman.

BROTHERLY AND SISTERLY LOVE: My sister, Maria, and me back in the day. Weren't we cute? We are just as close now as we were in that photo. *CREDIT: Judy Garrow*

GRADUATION DAY: My sister and me circa 2010, when I graduated from high school. This is when I first started to look deeper into the psychic abilities I had been pushing away for so long. This was a big milestone for me for both of those reasons.

NEW YORK, NEW YORK!: Shortly after going public with my work, I was invited to NYC to appear in a pay-per-view segment about developing psychic ability. My mom and I packed the car and headed to the city! My life was about to change. . . .

PSYCHIC HEADQUARTERS: My office opened soon after I published my first ebook, *The Secrets to Unlocking Your Psychic Ability.* That same year, I was featured in *Fashion & Fame* magazine. So many exciting chapters of my life were opening!

PSYCHIC ON AIR: My first radio tour started in Providence, RI. After giving live readings on air, I was asked to hold the first-ever psychic showcase premiere. It sold out in less than twenty-four hours.

PROUD MOM: I will never forget the feeling of seeing myself on a billboard in my hometown of Cranston, RI! My family all jumped into the car and took a field trip to see it in person. Of course, my mom couldn't help but take a picture.

SANTA CLAUS IS COMING!: Matching PJs is our newest family tradition! We all wear them on Christmas Eve. It is a blast! Left to right: Poppy, aka Grandpa Lou; my mom, Angela; my dad, Rod; and my sister, Maria.

FAMILY IS EVERYTHING: This was our last family picture before saying goodbye to my grandfather Lou. Yes, the one who thought I was a comedian instead of a medium. We have a family tradition of taking photos before saying goodbye to a loved one. I love to look back and smile at these special photos.

CREDIT: Diane Miller Photography | www.dianemillerphoto.com, dmillphoto@gmail.com

MATCH MADE IN HEAVEN: Alexa and me when I first brought her to Florida. This was shortly after I asked her to officially be my girlfriend.

WORLD TOUR: City-to-city and state-to-state, my tour grew from New England to worldwide! *CREDIT: Rachel Rodgers Photography*

UP CLOSE AND PERSONAL: I love being up close and personal when delivering messages. I can't help it. My mom always taught me to treat everyone like family, and I do. I love the people I meet and every second of what I do. *CREDIT: Rachel Rodgers Photography*

BEHIND THE SCENES: Alexa and me filming *Meet the Frasers* in Providence, RI. In this episode, we had a blast hosting one of Rhode Island's premier fashion shows.

QUIET ON THE SET!: Alexa and me filming interviews in the green-screen room, hamming it up. Can you tell we're camera shy? *CREDIT: Brian C. Dee |* *www.briandeedp.com*

TOOLS FOR LIFE

Never underestimate the power of your thoughts and words. It might be hard to imagine that your mind can manifest things—both good and bad—but it can! You attract what you spend your time on, so be sure you're focusing on the right things.

Want to protect yourself from dark energy? These simple tips can help keep you safe, wherever you are:

- For starters, don't seek out haunted houses or locations where negative things have happened. There's no point looking for trouble!

- Use your mind to visualize a protective cocoon of positivity and light surrounding you. Bring your "safe space" with you when you travel by packing a few photos and small items that represent love, family, and security.

- Warm up a hotel room, apartment, or office with photos, music, candles—anything to make the space feel like home. When you do, that good energy will push out any lingering negativity.

- When you're in an unfamiliar place where you don't feel comfortable, ask for help from a higher source. Say a little prayer or ask a loved one in spirit to watch over you.

• Let in the light—literally! Wherever you are, pull open the blinds and open the windows to let the sunlight and fresh air clear the space.

Certain places hold impressions and energy from past events, especially when pain and fear have been present for an extended period of time. But that energy can't hurt you if you are coming from a place of love and light.

CHAPTER 9

The Game of Telephone

When someone buys a ticket to a mediumship event or schedules a private reading, they expect to connect with a loved one on the other side. But calling upon spirit isn't like sending an email or a text. It's a three-way conversation. Spirit, medium, and the recipient each have an important part to play to make sure the message is relayed successfully.

First things first. Find the medium who's right for you. The medium must be able to connect you with a soul on the other side and translate his or her message in a way you can understand. He or she must speak the symbolic language of spirit, yet be able to convey what comes through in a way you can relate to.

There's no guarantee that a medium will bring through a message from a specific soul. My success rate is excellent, but spirit has to be willing. My job is to reach out to make a request for information, then do my best to translate that message. I tell my clients to see themselves as a critical part of the communications link, not a passive participant.

There are ways to maximize your chance of receiving the message you are meant to receive in a private or group session. It helps to know what's going on from the medium's perspective. Mediums connect with spirit in different ways. Some have visions, others hear voices. Many experience physical feelings or emotional impressions.

Here's what it's like for me. Messages come through really fast when I'm connecting to the other side. Words, pictures, dates, and symbols flash across my consciousness. At the same time, I experience physical feelings and sensations. There's a lot going on. I have to focus really hard to piece together what that particular soul is trying to communicate, a challenge for any medium. Luckily, spirit is expert at sending signals we can understand. Souls will even use people, places, and things within my own personal frame of reference to get their point across.

Sometimes it surprises me how well spirit knows me. For example, I have a friend who is the poster child for dysfunctional relationships. She always picks the wrong men, then spends too much time trying unsuccessfully to make things work. She's done this repeatedly since I've known her. Lately she's been showing up in some of my readings. Her appearance has become a symbol of the person's situation even though she has no relationship with the person I'm reading. She's kind of like mediumship shorthand for someone in a relationship going nowhere.

Mediums sometimes request specific information to help piece together an answer to a client's question. But this is a request, not a demand. It doesn't always work. Souls on the other side only communicate what they feel the recipient needs to know. They don't share everything. In other words, we can't validate every detail if the soul won't make that information available.

Sometimes the recipient of the message works harder than the medium. Some people tend to overthink things and want to do the interpreting for me. I was reading a woman the other day whose husband came through. Whenever I asked her to validate the messages I was getting, she kept saying, *I don't know. I don't know.* She couldn't seem to answer the simplest question. It seemed she'd barely known her husband.

Finally I said, *He said his name is Arthur.*

She was so excited. It turns out she'd lost three husbands and had been busy trying to figure out which one to apply the message to. It finally all made sense when she heard the name. She had been trying so hard to make the reading work for all three of her departed husbands, that it kept her from understanding the reading at all. It wasn't until Arthur told me his name that it clicked and she knew the reading was just about him.

MESSAGES COME FROM SPIRIT— NOT FROM ME

The best advice I can give you is to have an open mind and trust spirit when you're getting a reading. Open yourself up to listen and let the spirit people *talk*. Don't try to control the reading or you may block the message that's trying to come through.

People sometimes plan their reading in advance. Please, all you project managers out there, just relax! This is not something you can or should control.

It's perfectly normal to have someone in mind who you want

to hear from. It's also fine to bring Grandma's necklace to an event in your purse. But if you try to figure it all out in advance, you risk missing the message you really need to hear, from the soul you need to hear it from. Don't block that important message by being too rigid in your expectations.

FIRST AND FOREMOST IT'S THE MESSAGE THAT MATTERS

It's hard to let go and be open to the messages that may come through. I get it! I can be a control freak too. But that's not the best way to interact with spirit.

Would you call your husband on the phone, then tell him what to say? Hopefully not! In a good relationship, you want to hear what he has to say, not have him read from your script. The best way to connect with anyone, living or dead, is to really listen!

People will ask me questions to *test* the soul coming through.

Ask them who David is!

Ask where we went on our honeymoon?

They are seeking proof. But the soul you're connecting with isn't into playing games. They're eager to talk about things they feel you really need to know, not trivia. Don't waste time challenging the medium. Focus on the message being delivered. That's what matters.

If you're not open to counseling, even the best therapist can't help. It's the same with spirit messages. Let them communicate through the medium and be open to what comes through. Souls in heaven choose if they're going to come through or not. If I could control the process—who's going to come through and what they will say—it would have no meaning.

People ask me what they should do before a reading. They think they have to pray, look through photos, or talk to the soul beforehand. That's fine, but don't try too hard. You're not studying for an exam. You can't cram before a reading.

Help yourself, soul, and medium make the best possible connection by keeping these points in mind:

- Pick the right medium. Different psychics have different gifts. Some people want to talk to their pets and there are mediums who can do that. I love animals, but I prefer to focus on people and rarely talk to pets.

- Give the medium your trust and respect.

- Don't try to control things. Be open to whatever soul and message needs to come through.

- Don't be too literal. If you're looking for your mother and the details don't quite fit, maybe your mother-in-law is coming through instead. Open your mind to the possibilities.

- Come to a reading in a good mood. Happy and upbeat people attract spirit!

- If you're seeking guidance on something in particular, write it down. Spirit can see that piece of paper and will probably give me an answer before you share it with me. Genuine intentions come through to spirit and the right soul is likely to come through with the answer you need.

• Your intention needs to be to get the message, not prove a message right or wrong.

LET SPIRIT IN

Imagine if a family member or friend journeyed miles and miles to see you. Would you ignore their knock on the door? Now think of a soul coming through to you from the other side. Would you deny them a chance to get their message across?

DENIERS, READING SNATCHERS, AND NONRESPONDERS

I love it when I can deliver a message to someone ready to receive it. Hearing from a loved one who has passed can be a life-changing and healing experience. But some people put up unnecessary road-blocks when working.

Reading "deniers" are afraid or resistant. I used to be surprised by people who wouldn't accept a reading. I wasn't pulling them aside at the supermarket or surprising them at the movie theater! The people denying a reading had bought a ticket to one of my events, yet there they were rejecting the message spirit had for them.

I'm no longer surprised. People deny for several reasons. These range from shyness or shock at actually hearing from a loved one on the other side, to anger or resentment toward that particular soul, to fear of other people hearing what their loved one has to say.

I remember at one of my early events a woman was in the audience whose brother was coming through really strong. I could feel him in the area where she was sitting, but she denied even having a brother. The message had to be for her. She was the only one sitting in that row.

No, no, no. It must be for someone sitting here before.

I was confused, but she insisted she had no brother, so I moved on. Afterward she came up to me and said she actually did have a brother who'd passed. They'd been estranged for years before his death and she wasn't ready to hear from him. I explained her brother had come through to try to reconcile and I persuaded her to give him another chance. She booked a private reading. The brother came through with a lot of love and apologized for the fight they'd had before he died. She was able to accept his message in a private setting. I could tell it was very healing for her. Her energy felt so much lighter and happier after the reading.

READING SNATCHERS

Reading snatchers will do anything to try to make a reading fit. For instance, I'll be talking to a spirit named Patty in the front row. Someone in the back will pipe up.

That's my Steven!

Sometimes I can't resist making a joke.

Did Steven have boobs?

I've had people come up to me after an event and say, *Matt, every single message that came through was for me!* Of course the readings weren't all for them. They were just picking out pieces of other people's readings and trying to make them fit, like the stepsisters with Cinderella's glass slipper.

NONRESPONDERS

There are so many gracious people, but a few insist on making my job difficult.

It's never a good idea to talk too much when you're receiving a reading, but a little feedback is necessary to tell the medium he or she is on the right track.

All you need to do is say yes, no, or I don't know. But some people are dead silent, no pun intended. I like phone or Skype readings because I can focus better, but people have to respond or I'll think we've been disconnected!

Some people don't respond because they don't want to give the medium too much help and invalidate the reading. Sometimes friends have told them not to say anything.

Use a different name. Don't give the medium any clues.

People who get caught up in all that secrecy wind up closing themselves off to the message. Some even have friends schedule the reading to ensure I don't know a thing about them.

SUGGESTED VIDEO: Google "Matt Fraser Heart Stopping Reading" to watch a video of a woman who was a non-responder. I will never forget this reading. I brought through this woman's sister and she didn't say a word! After the segment, she hugged me and told me she was so in shock she was speechless. She couldn't believe her sister had actually come through!

Here are some common ways people block spirit messages:

• Getting nervous and talking over the medium so they can't deliver the message.

• Being so fixated on getting a message from one person, they don't recognize who is really coming through.

• Struggling to make the pieces fit when they don't.

• Not accepting a reading due to fear about what audiences or loved ones will think about revelations of drug use, suicide, affairs, etcetera.

Some people experience post-event remorse and email me after to tell me, *That was my father but I was afraid to speak up!*

I don't like to do readings the first year after someone has passed. People sometimes say spirit isn't ready, but it's not always the spirit that's the problem. The person who is grieving might not be ready, or their mind isn't clear. Doctors sometimes prescribe medications to deal with grief, closing the recipient off and making it difficult to get a message through.

It's never good to push too hard. People will come out into the lobby and try to get Mom to put in a good word with me. But when I'm onstage, the only words I receive are from spirit.

HOLDING ON TO PAIN AND GUILT

Guilt can block your ability to accept the message you're meant to hear.

I remember one particularly heartbreaking reading. A woman ran a red light and killed her son, who was thrown from the vehicle in the crash. People judged her from that moment on. It wasn't enough that she'd lost a son. She also had to deal with constant guilt and blame. Her husband divorced her. The in-laws disowned her. People accused her of not paying attention to the road and being on her phone. In reality, it was simply a tragic accident. People forgot how much she loved her son and how much pain she was in.

When her son came through, I could see the whole scene. She'd picked him up from school and was anxious to get home. As she rushed through an intersection a tractor trailer struck her car. Consumed by guilt and remorse, she'd blocked out the details of the accident and didn't really recall what happened. She'd hoped the accident hadn't been her fault. I had to tell her the truth—she had in fact run that red light and that was haunting her, but her son knew it was an accident.

It was hard for her to accept what I was telling her, that her son forgave her and couldn't bear to see her carry around such pain. It took a long time to get her to set aside her guilt and pain and hear his message from heaven. He loved her and needed her to let go of her guilt.

A MESSAGE OF HEALING

A man came to me. I could sense he was carrying a terrible burden. A few years earlier he'd encouraged his son, who'd recently gotten his license, to drive his younger sister to school. They'd gotten in an accident on the way and the daughter died.

The father kept his son out of jail but was very conflicted. He needed to blame someone for the accident. He felt his son murdered his daughter by his actions behind the wheel. The son enlisted into the military to escape his guilt and pain. The daughter came through and asked her father to forgive her brother and help him heal. It took many sessions, but the man was finally able to forgive his son. At one of our last sessions, a message came through that he would soon have a granddaughter to help ease the pain of losing his daughter. Knowing that it truly was an accident, and that his son was just a young and inexperienced driver, helped him to forgive his son. Knowing his daughter was okay and safe in heaven allowed him to keep moving forward and celebrate life.

STUCK IN THE AFTERLIFE

Your loved ones on the other side want you to live your life, but sometimes grief makes that difficult, especially when a person dies young and suddenly.

I met with a family who'd been very active in the community until their son passed away in his twenties from a heart problem that had gone undetected since birth. The mother and father were very involved in local charities, but the mother shut down after her son died. She dropped all her community work and became a recluse, only leaving her room to meet with psychics.

When I met her, I had a tough message from her son. He wasn't happy with the way she was living. She was stuck—never what spirit wants for you. Loved ones want to be there for you. They know it's best to go on living your life.

PSYCHICS ON SPEED DIAL

We talked about people who shut down and keep messages from coming through. However, it's also possible to be too open to spirit.

Some people are addicted to psychics. They become obsessive. They won't make a move without consulting their spiritual guru.

This feels to me like they're seeking guidance out of a lack of confidence or a fear of making a mistake. Sometimes they're just try-ing to get an answer from spirit that will persuade family or friends to stop questioning their life choices. For instance, some women consult a psychic to find some crumb of affirmation that will validate their choice to continue a relationship with a married man.

Is he my soul mate? Were we together in a past life? Will he ever leave his wife?

If they don't get the answer they want, they'll look for a second or third opinion from another medium. Or ask me the same question five different ways. Usually there's nothing I can say that will help. It's up to them to face the truth and accept the message.

YOU DON'T ALWAYS GET THE MESSAGE YOU WANT

A young man committed suicide after years of struggling with a severe social anxiety disorder. He was working with a therapist and trying different medications, but nothing helped. No matter what he tried, he was lonely and unhappy and couldn't connect with his fellow college students.

His parents came to me. They blamed a demanding professor and persisted in asking the same question over and over in different ways.

Was the professor hard on him?

Why did the teacher take things out on my son?

Why did this teacher target our son?

They needed a reason for the tragedy and were determined to blame the professor no matter what. I brought through a message from their son saying he had many secrets and his suicide had nothing to do with parents or teachers, but they went to another medium to get what they considered the *right* answer.

TOOLS FOR LIFE

Most people don't get too many opportunities to have a private reading or come to a demonstration of mediumship. It's understandable that they would put a lot of energy into trying to coax their deceased loved ones into showing up, but having too many expectations can sometimes push spirit away.

Here's how to make your experience the best it can be:

- Come to a reading or event with an open mind. It's okay to have a person in mind that you hope to hear from, or jot down a question you'd like answered, but beyond that it's best to release control and put your trust in the medium, and in spirit.

- Show up with an open heart. Remember that you're attending a joyful gathering that includes both the living and souls who have passed. Heaven wants you to be comforted and embrace the love that is being given through the messages.

- A mediumship demonstration is a group experience, so be respectful when someone else receives a message. Listen closely, because there are often messages that apply to more than one person in the audience.

- Be open to different souls connecting through the medium. Sometimes the person you most want to hear from stays in the background and lets another come through. Trust in the wisdom of spirit and know that you will receive the message you are meant to hear.

- More than one soul might come through in a reading. Be patient, and you might be part of the most amazing family reunion imaginable. Time is no barrier, and sometimes loved ones from multiple generations will appear together with insights and messages.

If you have a chance to attend a mediumship demonstration, I hope you'll take advantage of it. The healing and love that people experience at my events has a way of changing the way they view life and death forever!

CHAPTER 10

Soul Mates

People often call me an *old soul*. I'm pretty sure I know why.

Imagine being able to connect with souls on the other side and learn from their experiences. They have amazing clarity as they look down and review the time they spent on earth. I feel blessed to benefit from their insights and try to apply those lessons to my own life. Every chance I get I share these insights with the people around me.

When you talk to heaven on a regular basis, you begin to realize what really matters in life. Long story short, what matters most is love. There are many kinds of love and all contribute to your happiness, health, and fulfillment. The more you can experience love the better, whether it's with a spouse, child, pet, or friend. You name it, it's all good!

But what does everyone want most? Yes, you guessed it! Just about everyone I meet is looking for a soul mate.

HOW CAN YOU FIND
YOUR SOUL MATE?

Everyone has a soul mate, a twin flame, someone your heart inter-twines with at the deepest level.

Some people believe soul mates have shared past lives. I don't know about that, but I do know they carry that soul connection with them into the next world.

It's totally possible and normal to enjoy a long, happy, and pro-ductive relationship with someone who is not your soul mate. You can be married and have children together without a problem, but that relationship's place is in the here and now. It might not go any further.

Don't worry too much about missing out on your great love. You might not reconnect with your husband or wife in heaven, but you will surely reconnect with your soul mate.

Here's what I mean. An eighty-year-old woman came to an event. Her husband came through and she was happy to hear from him, but then another man stepped forward with so much love for her. Boy, was she excited to hear from him!

Were you married twice?

No, the second man was my boyfriend, whom I met after my hus-band died. I loved my husband, but the relationship with my boyfriend was really special and he's who I want to spend the afterlife with.

People are in relationships for reasons of economics, business, children, and more. Sometimes it works, sometimes it doesn't. Sometimes people want to get divorced but then the spouse gets sick or something else conspires to make them stay.

Relationships are complicated. It helps to remember the one you're with on earth is not necessarily the one you'll be with on the other side.

REUNITED IN THE AFTERLIFE . . .

I've run into many people who regret they let their one true love slip away. Maybe they were preoccupied at the time or stuck in another relationship. Sometimes bad timing, fear of commitment, or plain old practicality gets in the way of a soul mate connection.

Don't worry. You may have missed your chance at true love in this life, but the universe has a plan. Even if you've married more than once or had dozens of relationships, you'll reconnect with your soul mate in the afterlife.

If you are sure you found your soul mate but the relationship ends for whatever reason, know that they will come back into your life when the time is right. The universe will bring that person back to you if it's meant to be. But don't put your life on hold. Stay open to new experiences and relationships. Remember, if it's meant to be it will be.

My grandpa's story illustrates this perfectly. He was crazy about a girl he met when he was sixteen. He wanted to be with her in the worst way. He felt she was his soul mate. She turned him down for another man. She wanted someone older. She went on to meet her husband. Grandpa was brokenhearted but eventually met my grandma Mary, whom he married.

Both my grandpa and his soul mate had beautiful families and children, though they remained far apart. Almost fifty years later both spouses passed away around the same time. As fate would have it, my grandpa and his soul mate ran into each other years later at the grocery store and picked up where they'd left off as teens. They never regretted their marriages but were thankful to connect decades later. I know they were meant to be together, but only after they experienced what they needed to experience. I may be a little biased, though, since I wouldn't be here if they hadn't married other people and lived separate lives.

It's like that Richard Bach quote. *If you love something, set it free. If it comes back, it's yours. If it doesn't, it never was.*

Be open to all kinds of love and trust in the divine plan.

Sometimes people lose a spouse and are afraid to date again. They're afraid to risk not being reconnected with their husband or wife in the afterlife. It doesn't work that way. New people cross your path for many reasons. Sometimes the person on the other side is the one pulling the strings and making things happen.

I did a reading for a woman who dated her brother-in-law after her husband passed. She felt a ton of guilt and her in-laws were pretty freaked out by the new relationship. The husband came through to tell her he'd orchestrated the whole thing. He'd put his brother in her path so they could ease each other's grief and loneliness. He wanted them to be happy and looked forward to reuniting with his wife in heaven.

I did another reading for a young woman who'd lost a boyfriend tragically. He'd died in her arms and she still carried the pain. She often wondered about the life they could have had if he'd been able to keep his promise and stay off drugs. He came through and said he loved her and they would have had a family and still been together if he hadn't died. But since that wasn't in the cards, he wanted her to move on and live her life.

It was a beautiful reading. He came through with so much love for her. It was very healing. The woman sitting next to her said, *That can't be true. They wouldn't be together. She's a lesbian now.*

She'd found comfort in a relationship with a woman after her boyfriend passed. He was supportive of her journey. Love is love. I believe that if they're soul mates they will ultimately be together.

People come into our lives for different reasons. You can't just sit around waiting for your soul mate, but that doesn't mean he or she isn't out there. People are so afraid of not being able to find a mate that they often settle for what's comfortable.

WAITING FOR "THE ONE"

Years ago, when I was just starting out as a psychic medium, I dated a girl in the medical field for a year or two. She was really nice and we had lots in common because of my EMT work, but there was no spark.

We finally realized something was missing—we just didn't complete each other. It was hard to separate. We liked each other a lot, but I knew she wasn't *the one*. The relationship took a lot of work because we weren't really compatible. I'm super neat; she was messy. I'm an omnivore; she was vegan. We didn't try to change each other but it was difficult, and I worried about breaking up because we had such a strong friendship and so many memories together.

It was scary, but we decided to separate. My grandma Jean gave me the best advice. She told me to take a break from other people. Learn to spend time by myself and enjoy taking a walk, sitting in a coffee shop, or decorating the house. The right person will come along when the time is right.

I started attending parties and events alone. I met new friends and had many great conversations. I was enjoying things on my own terms, learning a lot, and rediscovering myself. I also spent more time with clients and family, and strengthened ties with my sister.

Before I met Alexa, I created a vision board of what I wanted in a relationship. A few years earlier, I'd judged a Massachusetts beauty pageant. I was so impressed by the girls' beauty, talent, intelligence, and willingness to be in the spotlight that I put a crown on my board. I added pictures representing someone with style who enjoyed socializing and had dark hair and dark eyes. Then I put the board under my bed and forgot about it.

I was dating and meeting really nice girls, but there was no soul mate connection. One night in bed after an event, spirit was still in my head. I couldn't sleep. Scrolling Instagram, I saw a girl on my feed who looked happy and beautiful. I didn't know her, but I clicked on her photo. I have no idea why she showed up on my feed. I don't remember who followed whom. But I saw she'd been Miss Rhode Island 2017 so I sent her a note of congratulations. We messaged back and forth. Then I invited her for coffee at a local café. My heart started pounding as soon as I saw her. We had planned to meet for fifteen minutes, but we were there for an hour. I hated to leave but I had a meeting. She said she hoped to see me again.

I didn't want her to know that I was so into her. I walked her to her car and tried to play it cool, but already I was dying to see her again!

I invited her to dinner the following week. She said yes. I got all dressed up and drove to her house. We stayed out 'til three a.m. just chatting. Talking to her was effortless—she loved everything I loved.

People think I live a lavish life, but I prefer to hang out at home with Alexa, watch Netflix, and eat takeout. Being with her has made me realize relationships don't have to be that hard. If it's too much of an uphill battle, maybe it's not meant to be. When my clients have issues with boyfriends—or are obsessed with getting someone back after a breakup—I ask them to imagine navigating finances and children with someone with whom everything is a struggle.

I'm amazed at how compatible Alexa and I are. Neither of us likes to party and we're both super close to family. We have the same views and find it easy to live together. We support each other's careers. I try to eat healthy—not easy for me—when she's preparing for a pageant. She can recognize when I'm in a daze as I receive information from spirit, and she doesn't take it personally. Alexa understands what it's like to be in the spotlight and how committed I am to what I do. I like seeing Alexa achieve her dreams. She feels the same for me. Even our parents get along.

Everything went so well from the start. We were both in a good place mentally and emotionally to start a relationship. We'd both been with other people we weren't compatible with and were ready for this. I guess it helps that both our careers are a little unusual. We're both misunderstood a lot.

WHEN YOU LOSE YOUR SOUL MATE WHAT HAPPENS?

Your true love is called a soul mate for a reason. You will reconnect in heaven. But no one is meant to spend their life alone. Until you are reunited, your loved one will send people to be with you. They don't want you to be alone.

We had a neighbor who lost her husband, a nice, supportive man who cared for his wife when she was sick and helped with her business. The husband died unexpectedly. She was devastated and was sure she'd never be with another man. Then by happenstance she met Tony, who'd also lost a spouse he adored. That's what brought them together.

It's not your typical relationship. They're both still in love with their deceased spouses and always talk about their soul mates in heaven. However, while they are still here on earth, this new love is helping them heal.

A friend who was painting their house observed them sharing stories about the loved ones who'd passed and thought it was crazy, but they both appreciate having someone who understands how they feel and isn't jealous.

In matters of the heart we find what we need. Everyone's different!

SUGGESTED VIDEO: Google "Matt Fraser Brings Husband Through" to watch a reading of a woman reconnecting with her husband who passed on. I love seeing tears of joy when someone is reconnected with a soul mate. You can clearly see the impact.

TOOLS FOR LIFE

As a psychic medium, I have the unique opportunity to learn about life, love, redemption, and regret from souls who can look back on their lives with twenty-twenty hindsight.

I've learned that what matters most is love. When souls pass over, they stay connected to the people they loved. Do they haunt the office or hang around their old sports car? Usually not. Their love toward their spouse, children, extended family, friends, and pets is what endures.

The dead have taught me that in order to live a happy life that you can look back on without regrets, you have to focus on love. To live your life fully, be present in your relationships and make them a priority. Here are some things to keep in mind:

- Let your family and friends know how much you care for them while you are here on earth. I'll do my best to get the message to them after you pass—but why not tell people how you feel before you need to get a medium involved?

- Looking for your soul mate? Here's what worked for me. I created a vision board with images of the life I wanted, including the type of person I wanted to be with. Many of the things I put on my board manifested—including the love of my life, Alexa!

- If you have lost or been separated from someone you believe was your soul mate, know that you will reconnect again in heaven. It's natural to miss them and be sad, but trust the divine plan.

If you're grieving the loss of a loved one, this might comfort you. You will see them again! When your own soul is about to depart, you will be greeted by loved ones already in heaven—the same souls who have been watching over you since they passed. Love never dies.

CHAPTER 11

Heaven, Transitions, and the Afterlife

t's normal to harbor fear about the unknown. For most people, mediums excluded, death is about as *unknown* as it gets.

Being somewhat of an expert, let me reassure you no one enters heaven alone. There are loved ones there to greet and guide you. Even long lost pets are there, loyal to the end and beyond!

You don't have to wait until your actual passing to see your heavenly transition team. Some people see loved ones standing by their bed when they are dying or in a coma. There are always family members and loved ones there to help them transition home.

YOUR OWN VERSION OF HEAVEN

I haven't been to heaven, but as a medium I get glimpses. The souls I connect with share! Based upon what I've seen so far, I believe heaven is an energy space and we all create our own version.

For a mountain climber, heaven is a place of magnificent peaks. A person who loves the ocean will see waves all around.

Earlier I shared how my beloved grandmother often appeared to me after she passed. On one of these visits she showed me a glimpse of heaven, a beautiful place with golden buildings. I don't know if that's what Grandma was experiencing or if that's how she chose to show it to me.

The idea that we each experience our own personal version of heaven is hard to grasp. You have to let go of traditional ideas that it's a physical place. It's not. When you transition you leave your body behind and become pure soul energy. It's a whole different state of consciousness. It's a lot like dreaming.

When you sleep you create your own dreams no one else can see. Heaven is like that too, just better because you're sharing it with loved ones. It's like living in a big apartment building. Everyone is in one place, but the inside of each unit is completely different and a direct reflection of that person and their personality.

Another thing that's hard to wrap your head around is that there's no time in heaven. And boundaries from the physical world are gone. You may meet people you never met in life. You'll know their name.

When people attend an event, they usually have someone in mind they hope to get a message from. But sometimes they hear from someone else whom they didn't know they were connected to. Unexpected readings can be powerful and life-changing. Souls can come through we never met in life. Unborn babies can come through who felt the love their mother felt for them in the womb. Parents connect with children they gave up for adoption.

COMFORT FROM HEAVEN

Souls who come through often try to describe heaven in interesting ways. They want so badly for us to understand.

A mother came through who said her daughter had recently been going through old photo albums and became sad when she realized everyone in the photos was dead. The mother pointed out to me that what her daughter was doing was a bit like what heaven is like—reliving memories with loved ones who've passed.

When a friend of mine was young she chased a ball into the street and was hit by a car. She was in a coma for several weeks. Doctors feared she wouldn't make it. When my friend recovered, she said she never realized she was in a coma. Her friend, who'd passed away a few years earlier from illness, was with her the whole time. They played video games just like they'd done when they were alive. It was like a dream. Before she came to, the friend told her she had to wake up to say hello to her family. It wasn't freaky or scary. Spirit only comes to you in a way you're comfortable with.

It occurred to me that the classic white tunnel of light we associate with near-death experiences might have been too scary for a child, so her friend chose another way to help her.

One valuable thing I've learned as a medium is that death isn't something to be afraid of. It's not the end; it's just a passage to another place where we remain connected to loved ones who are still alive. Spirit doesn't want us to be afraid and will guide us every step of the way.

No one enters heaven kicking and screaming, even those determined to hang on to life with both hands. My grandfather was supposed to pass three months before he finally did, but he kept willing himself to live. He needed a little extra time. His body was broken and hurting, but his heart wasn't ready. In his final days he told me he could see his girlfriend who'd passed. He told me he thought he was hallucinating. I explained she was coming through to guide him. When he was finally ready, he passed peacefully. His old girlfriend and soul mate was there to help him transition.

PACK YOUR BAGS FOR HEAVEN

Getting to heaven is like going through TSA. To pass over you have to go through a life review.

As souls transition, they become aware of the influence they've had on others while they were alive. They can see the people they've hurt and those they've helped. Some souls take longer than others to complete this review and progress to the next level. They might even be given tasks to perform to help raise their vibration. It's a bit like AA. You have to acknowledge what you've done and make any necessary amends before moving on.

One thing spirit has made clear—when you transition to heaven you have to let go of any heavy emotions dragging you down. It's like passing through a water filter. Your energy has to be clear and light to pass through. You have to forgive. Imagine if we all crossed over, dragging along our resentments and negative energy. Talk about baggage! Heaven wouldn't be heaven anymore.

TRADITIONS THAT EASE
THE PAIN OF SEPARATION

So many people feel sad at a loved one's passing because they won't be able to attend a particular milestone like a christening or college graduation. But there's never a right time to let go of someone you love. If they hang on 'til Christmas, you'll hope they'll stick around 'til New Year's, Valentine's Day, Easter, or that July Fourth barbecue!

But there are ways to ease the pain of letting go. A recent experience illustrates this.

A young woman came to an event. She looked the picture of health. Her mother who'd passed a few years earlier told me her daughter was very sick. She'd been watching over her during treatments. The daughter came up to me after the event and asked me to tell her about death and dying. She was terrified of dying because she wanted to be there for her two teenage daughters as they reached important milestones.

I had to help her. We arranged to meet one-on-one a week or so later. I explained what heaven was like, but what she really wanted to know was how to reach her daughters. I recommended she devise signs she could share with her girls—pennies or rainbows or anything her daughters could look for that would tell them their mother was okay. So she sat down with her daughters to put together different words, songs, and signs to watch for after she passed. That way she could send specific messages when they were sad, celebrating, or just missing her. It put her mind at ease to know she would have a way to support them as they grew up.

About two years later the mother of two young women in the audience came through.

I feel I know her, I said, but couldn't place her.

They told me she'd had a reading with me, and they'd come that night because they knew that if she would come through to anyone it would be me. Their mother let me know our plan had worked. The daughters thanked me for helping her set up the signs before she passed. It made her passing easier, and has given them comfort over the years.

GOD GAVE HER EXTRA TIME

I did a reading for a woman who started crying as soon as her mother came through. Her mother had been very practical and always worked hard. She always took care of everyone else, never herself.

The daughter decided to take her mother on a special trip to celebrate her eightieth birthday. Although the mother objected, the daughter insisted. Other family members came too. Everyone had a great time relaxing and sightseeing and spending time together.

On the flight home, she thanked her daughter for a great vacation.

These have been the best days of my life. I just need to close my eyes for a minute. She died holding her daughter's hand.

Instead of feeling good she'd given her mother one last special gift, the daughter felt guilty the trip had killed her. She couldn't forgive herself. Her mother came through at the reading to tell her daughter she'd had a heart condition and had been given a little extra time to enjoy her first vacation. Without it she would have died earlier.

The daughter had somehow intuited her mother didn't have much time left and made her last moments special. Now she could enjoy cherished memories of her mother and beautiful photos of their time in Aruba without feeling guilty

HOW IMPORTANT ARE THOSE FINAL HOURS?

People feel they have to be there for their loved one's last breath. When you have shared so many moments and expressed your love over the years, there's nothing special about that last breath—especially to the person passing.

Some people prefer to slip away when you're not there so as to spare you the pain. Your loved one will tell you what they want. They might know they can't let go while you're there, so they will hang on.

Some people are big on funerals, which can be stressful when you have to make all the arrangements while dealing with your grief and loss. I've planned my own funeral so that my loved ones won't have to organize it and can enjoy the service.

From what I've heard from spirit, the deceased are often present at their funeral and wake. But don't let that worry you! They're not there to judge the music or the food, or keep tabs on who shows up. They're watching over their loved ones. Their only concern is how the family is coping.

I personally have a hard time at funerals. I have difficulty getting emotional about it because I know the body isn't what's important. What matters is the soul.

People are more energy than anything else. After you die that energy leaves your body like *Elvis leaving the building*. I find it more meaningful to feel the person's presence, look at photos, and revisit memories of them when they were still alive. I know viewing the body one last time can give some people closure, but for me it's an empty shell lying in a box.

You might wonder how people can attend their own funeral. Many mediums say people who pass don't come back right away. It's true that it can take time for a loved one to come through to a medium. That doesn't mean he or she isn't with you! It takes time to learn to connect with a medium and communicate that way, but that doesn't mean they aren't there watching over you. It just means that they are learning the new language that they will need to use to communicate with you.

Loved ones might take their time coming through to a medium for another reason. As I mentioned earlier, Grandma would come through to me but not to her daughter. She was worried Mom would focus too much on spirit and disconnect from her own life. Spirit doesn't want you getting stuck as you try to connect. It wants you to focus on living.

LOOKING BACK—HINDSIGHT
IS TWENTY-TWENTY

Sometimes our loved ones don't make it easy for us when they pass. Grandpa always said, *Don't cry and get upset when I go. Live your life!*

I feel blessed to know he wanted me to be happy, but it's not that way for everyone.

Sometimes souls are desperate to have their message heard. They may regret how they behaved at the end. Sometimes they want loved ones to know they were out of their minds with pain when they blamed a loved one or were angry and ungrateful.

I've seen so many souls come through with apologies to the living.

For instance, one woman's mother immediately came through to apologize for making her daughter feel guilty for putting her in assisted living.

A bipolar man came through who said he wished he could take back the vicious letter he'd left his wife, blaming her for his suicide. He regretted blaming her. Now, looking back, he knew his problems had nothing to do with her.

An older woman begged me to let her son know she should never have pressured him to spend so much time with her and neglect his own children. She realized in her life review that she'd been selfish.

Souls in heaven are not vindictive. They can see past actions more clearly from the other side and let go of grudges and negative feelings when they go through their life review. Their main goal is to help loved ones on earth be happy. They want them to feel their love. That's not to say they're always unconditionally accepting. They might send a message guiding you or even offering constructive criticism, but that message is sent with your best interests at heart.

Sometimes a parent will come through at an event with stern advice to children that they need to treat each other better and not squabble over the inheritance. The loved one wants to help those left behind live their best life and maintain good relationships.

Some people feel bad because they can't fulfill a loved one's dying wish. They might not be able to keep the family home or are forced to sell some antiques, jewelry, or other treasures. Souls that have passed often come through with encouraging words that let surviving family members know they've already let material possessions go.

When I get messages on this topic, I don't pick up on concern about material things. But many do share regrets about cutting people out of wills or other decisions that have needlessly hurt relationships between the living.

I remember a difficult reading with a woman who had been shocked to learn she'd been cut out of her mother's will. They'd enjoyed a wonderful relationship, but the mother had struggled with dementia at the end. She expressed regret and her daughter experienced some emotional healing, but a medium can't help you get reinstated in your mother's will!

We think of heaven as a wonderful place, but you have to be deceased to get there. Think of it this way—heaven is just a phase of your existence, like childhood or old age, each unfolding in its own time. When you put fear of the unknown aside and are truly present in each phase, it's easier to accept that heaven will be a beautiful resting place when your time comes.

> **SUGGESTED VIDEO:** Google "Matt Fraser What Happens When You Die" to watch a video of what happens after you enter into the spirit world.
>
> **SUGGESTED VIDEO:** Google "Matt Fraser 10 Secrets of the Afterlife" to learn more secrets about life after death.

TOOLS FOR LIFE

When I deliver messages from heaven at a live event, I can feel the shift as the audience starts to rethink their perspective on death and dying. I feel like I'm doing something positive to help people get over their fear of death by proving to them that death is not the end, but rather a transition.

Over the years I've heard the same themes over and over from souls on the other side. Their insights have changed my own feelings about loss, grief, and dying—I hope they give you something to think about too:

- First, no one dies alone. Loved ones are with every single person who passes to welcome them to heaven.

- If you regret not being beside a loved one at the moment they pass, please let go of that guilt and know that they are always met by other loved ones, friends, and even pets who went to heaven before them.

- Everyone has their own version of heaven. Spirit has shown me very different visions of heaven, and no two are alike. So if Hollywood's image of heaven doesn't appeal to you, don't worry when you die, you become pure energy, and the heaven that you perceive will be a perfect match for you.

- The dead attend their own funerals. While attending a funeral I have seen the departed loved one watching over their family and friends, sending them comfort and love.

• Live your best life on earth. Hold on to the positive memories and experiences after your loved one has transitioned to heaven. Their fondest wish is for you to be happy and enjoy your life experiences.

Death is a transition into pure spirit energy and a very pure state of consciousness. There is no reason to fear death, because love is eternal and your loved ones are always with you.

CHAPTER 12

Loose Ends and Unfinished Business

Everyone faces death differently. In a perfect world most people would like to leave this earth with everything tied up in a bow, but that's not always how it works.

If you know in advance when you're going to die or if you're especially well organized, you may have the opportunity to get your affairs in order. Lots of people, myself included, plan their own funeral and put videos and letters aside for loved ones.

But sometimes life and death have other plans. People die suddenly or are not in their right mind when they pass. Often they're in denial and don't want to face reality. When the inevitable happens, loved ones may be left with unanswered questions as to what the dearly departed was feeling when they passed or, more important, what to do about funeral arrangements, pets, and possessions. Not an event goes by when I don't get these types of questions from relatives.

IS MY LOVED ONE HAPPY
AND HEALTHY IN HEAVEN?

I'm usually able to put people's minds at ease regarding the afterlife, which lets everyone leave behind illnesses, handicaps, and impairments, and enter heaven lighter and happier.

If you live to a ripe old age, you're bound to experience some aches and pains. But once you pass on, you leave behind any ailments you had in life.

When we die we go through a life review. All the years of our life are played back and we're able to see those we've helped, those we've hurt, the consequences of our decisions, and the changes we should have made. We also see those who helped us and made a difference in our lives. Many times we see things people have done for us that we never even knew about.

Life review gives souls closure and a chance to make amends by helping and guiding those they may have wronged in life.

I NEVER GOT TO SAY GOOD-BYE!

After people die, their focus shifts to those left behind. When they die suddenly, they may be especially concerned for the welfare of wives, children, or friends left behind. They remember times spent together in life, regardless of what happened in their last moments.

The living feel guilty if they didn't make it to someone's bedside when they were dying. But trust me. The dead don't spend their time worrying about that!

I WISH I COULD TAKE IT ALL BACK

Those who are old, sick, in pain, or afraid of dying, often say things they don't mean. Sometimes they blame other people for their passing. That's understandable. But when they have their life review, they can see clearly the effect those words had on those around them. The first thing many souls tell me is how much they regret their final hours.

I had a man come though who'd committed suicide after struggling to reenter civilian life following his return from war. He couldn't get his relationship with his wife on track. They were sleeping separately and on the brink of divorce. He left a note blaming his wife for his pain.

In his life review it became crystal clear his wife wasn't the problem. He'd needed more help dealing with trauma he'd experienced in battle. When he came through, the first thing he wanted to do was apologize to his wife. He'd been taking pain medication and had blamed her for something that wasn't her fault. Looking back he could see all the love she'd shown him. His soul was waiting for the chance to tell her how wrong he'd been to blame her and that he wished her nothing but love and happiness.

Not only could he see his own actions and what had really caused his pain, he could also see the residual effects on his wife, who was weighed down with guilt and feeling blamed by his family.

His wife felt so much better after receiving this message. She'd been burdened by the belief that she was responsible for his death and had felt a heavy weight as she imagined him looking down and blaming her. It was like a cloud over her head that kept her from experiencing happiness and moving on. Hearing that her husband no longer blamed her finally gave her closure.

TELL ME MORE ABOUT THE LIFE REVIEW!

People always want to know more about the life review and what souls really see. The answer is they see everything! How can a life review cover so many years? I imagine it's like a dream where you see everything from different angles in a few seconds, but it seems like a lifetime.

WILL SUICIDE KEEP
YOU OUT OF HEAVEN?

Suicides are particularly painful for those left behind. One of the questions I hear most from people who've lost a loved one to suicide is will it keep them out of heaven?

What I hear from souls who've come through to me after committing suicide is that they go through a life review just like anyone who died of any other cause. Sometimes those who've taken their own life get a *do-over* that can take different forms—

for instance, through reincarnation. I believe they now have the opportunity to do God's work with a fresh start here on earth or in heaven.

One common message from souls who've ended their own lives is that they didn't realize help was available until after they passed. Pain, depression, loss, and addiction made it impossible to see a way out. Often they see suicide wasn't a conscious choice. They may have been suffering from mental illness and couldn't help themselves. They thought people were judging them or had abandoned them. In hindsight they realized they were not in a position to accept the help that was being offered.

I find souls of those who've committed suicide are driven to help prevent others from making the same mistake, which is truly doing God's work. Sometimes they *pull strings* like bringing it to the family's attention via divine intervention to put people and resources in the path of those who may be thinking of ending their life.

Suicide is not the end, and not as black and white as you might believe. Based on what I've learned from years of talking to spirit, these souls can now see things more clearly and redeem themselves by helping others from the other side.

ADDICTION

Addiction can affect those left behind similarly. Often the survivors feel shame because of what people think. But the feeling that death could have been prevented can be worse.

I find that people who have passed due to an overdose come through with a great concern for others. They hope their death will help others get clean. Young people sometimes experiment with drugs because they feel invincible. They don't realize the potential consequences. Heaven affords many chances and wake-up calls, but if people choose to ignore them, they may die before their time. I believe that the universe gives us many chances. Family and friends try to intervene. Doctors and paramedics bring some back from an overdose with quick, appropriate treatment. And rehab provides a chance to start over. But ultimately, if these interventions and efforts to get clean don't work and the person passes, they see the choices they made and are determined to help others make different choices. They might try to influence another addict directly or contact a family member and alert them to the problem.

Sometimes one unfortunate experiment with drugs or alcohol can be the last. Others who die from alcohol and drugs have ignored many wake-up calls along the way. It's really not that different from a heart attack. Most people don't drop dead of a heart attack without warning. Their physician likely told them to lose weight, exercise, and take medication. In the end it was their choice to get healthy.

A foster mother came to me for a reading, hoping to connect with a foster child who'd passed. She had fostered many children, but this child had been her first and she'd formed a deep attachment to him. The boy had grown up around addicts and had battled addiction himself. She helped him get help. But after three years of sobriety he got back into drugs. She had no idea he'd started using again, and the realization made her question everything. It hurt her so much to think she'd saved him only to discover he'd gone back on drugs and died.

She came to me questioning her ability to foster and help children. He came through and told her she'd done right by him and had given him a second chance. He would have passed years earlier without her influence. He urged her to keep working with children.

She came to me upset at how she'd failed him. His message helped her feel better and to continue to foster more children.

When an addict dies, we often second-guess ourselves and struggle with pain and guilt. When we continue to move forward and live life as best we can, we help those who've passed to redeem themselves.

WHEN YOUR LOVED ONE ISN'T THEMSELVES WHEN THEY PASS

Many with Alzheimer's or other forms of dementia are able to look back and see how family members cared for them even though they didn't realize it at the time. Life review helps them see things more clearly and rationally.

An entire family came to an event I held in Newport. They wanted to help their mother get in touch with her late husband. She kept saying she saw him. They kept reminding her he'd died, thinking her Alzheimer's was making her delusional. The woman wasn't delusional at all when it came to her husband, who came through to confirm his wife knew he'd passed and even remembered who came to his funeral! Being so close to death herself, she'd actually been seeing her husband, whose spirit came to visit regularly. His soul wanted to watch over her and be there when she passed. This elderly woman was deeply confused in some ways, but seeing her husband clearly brought her comfort. My reading let her family know what was really going on and put their minds at ease.

SECRETS AND LIES

Mothers tell their children to always wear clean underwear in case they get in an accident. It's the same with death, except we often die at less-than-opportune times, leaving secrets and other unfinished business for loved ones to discover.

A man came to an event who'd been adopted by parents who wouldn't disclose anything about his biological family. He was their only son and they were afraid of losing him. After they passed away, he was left with nobody. He tracked his biological family down and discovered his brother had also passed and now he had no chance of ever knowing him. His adopted parents came through to say they wished they'd let him know his biological family so he could have met his brother before he died.

This particular reading was helpful to everyone in the audience. I bet there wasn't anyone who heard this reading who didn't leave with more awareness of how fear and worry can prevent us from telling someone a truth they have a right or need to hear.

Nearly half the readings that come through relate in some way to unfinished business—whether from addiction, suicide, sudden death, or secrets left behind. These souls are the most desperate to come through and clear the air. There are so many lessons to be learned from readings like this, which is why people get so much value from attending a mediumship event, even if they don't get a personal reading.

SUGGESTED VIDEO: Google "Matt Fraser Not Getting To Say Good-bye Video" to watch a woman receive a reading and reconnect with her brother who had passed away unexpectedly while her plane was landing at JFK International Airport.

TOOLS FOR LIFE

I want to share with you some universal themes I have learned from spirit. Our time on earth is designed for learning lessons, and the souls who are looking back on their lives make wonderful mentors for the living.

Here are some things the dead want you to know:

- Don't worry about them! They are no longer in pain; they are not suffering from a physical or mental impairment any longer; their journey in heaven is happy and they are filled with peace.

- Be mindful of your actions while you're alive. Kindness matters. Be aware now of how you behave and become more compassionate in your thoughts and actions with others. During the transition process, you will have a full life review—where you will look back on and understand your life, intentions, and interactions with others. You will see the effect that your words and actions had on people you encountered. You can think of it as a way to understand and experience closure from your earthly life, which allows your soul to grow and evolve.

- Spirit messages are never intended to hurt the living. Many messages from heaven are given to clear up a misunderstanding or to right a wrong that was unresolved in life. It is always done to bring clarity and comfort to the audience member.

If I could sum up everything spirit wants you to know, it would come down to this: be kind, be loving, and don't be afraid. Your loved ones in heaven are watching over you and sending you love.

CHAPTER 13

Lights, Camera, Spirit!

When I first rediscovered my gift, I never imagined I might someday be a famous medium. The idea of receiving national attention seemed like a fantasy. Looking back on the days when I was doing readings for ten dollars in the back of the hair salon—just a few years ago—I cannot believe how far I have come.

I love doing this work and delivering messages. I never felt that I needed a TV show or fame. I really didn't think of mediumship as a profession. It was more like a calling—something I did because I loved helping people heal from their grief after losing someone they loved. I believe God gave me this ability to heal the pain of losing a loved one and share the universal wisdom that messages from spirit can bring. I love reminding people that there is life after death, and your loved ones are always with you.

In the beginning of my career, I worked two jobs just to fund my mediumship. I remember some days not even breaking even after paying for gas, travel, and expenses.

One day I received a call that changed everything. A television producer had learned about me and wanted me to join a casting call for a psychic show that was in development. I was hesitant at first but decided to go for it.

I couldn't help but to think "They want me!?"

This call happened years ago, when I was just starting out. Back then, I had not been on TV much, and really didn't understand the TV world. But I was ready to learn!

I decided that I would say yes and see where heaven was leading me. I went through the process of signing contracts, and several meetings later I realized that this was a new dream. It immediately made me think bigger. I wanted to step out of my shell and be an inspiration to the world. I felt as if the sky was the limit. I could now use my ability to reach and speak to people worldwide. I didn't have to hide my gift like my grandmother had, I could bring inspiration to the world and demystify the realm of psychic ability.

I was so excited. I was being told that I would be the next psychic sensation and that soon the messages I was delivering would receive national attention.

I looked forward to the day when people would actually start to hear about me and imagined what it would be like to be in people's homes on TV, helping and healing. I felt like I didn't even deserve it, but I trusted that heaven was leading me in the right direction and that this was where I was supposed to be.

Everything about it just seemed right. I spent so much time dreaming about my future and being able to leave my job to do deliver messages full-time.

Each week there was a different meeting. I was asked to send videos of my work, client testimonials, and was even invited to give readings to executives in New York City and meet with producers. I remember walking into the room nervous and a little intimidated. They wanted readings on the spot to know that I was "real." My publicist, Imal, looked at me and said, "You can do this. Go in there and just let loose. Don't hold back; tell them everything that you hear and see."

I walked in and suddenly the fear subsided. I looked around the room and didn't even notice the producers. All I saw was their loved ones who had passed away, standing behind them, waiting for me to deliver their messages. I knew what I had to do, and heaven was there to help me.

Immediately to my right was a man who had lost his fiancée to a sudden and aggressive cancer. She was in the room, letting him know how much she loved him. She was thanking him for sitting beside her and hugging her while she took her last breath. She even knew that he was struggling with the idea of selling the house because he didn't want to let go of anything that was connected to her.

Next to him was a woman who had lost her godmother unexpectedly. The family had no idea what had caused the woman's death, and the autopsy was inconclusive. They feared it was murder and that she had been poisoned. The woman came through to say that her heart had been weak and it had just stopped. She wanted her family to know that she was sorry about how they had found her, but that she was at peace with her cat that had passed.

The souls kept coming through, and one by one each of the producers was reconnected with someone they knew and loved. The readings could not have been more accurate. I was getting the chills myself as spirit kept whispering names, dates, and personal information that nobody could have known or looked up. The people in the room went from being skeptical and intimidating to experiencing tears, love, and healing. At the end of the meeting, instead of handshakes, there were hugs and thank-yous.

Weeks and weeks went by. I waited on the edge of my seat until one day I received a call that shook me. I was told that production decided to drop the whole idea of developing a psychic medium show. They felt there wasn't enough interest in the topic.

They thanked me for their readings and asked if they could recommend me to friends and family. Just like that, the door of opportunity was closed.

I had been given what I thought was a once-in-a-lifetime opportunity, only to be turned down.

I remember going to bed one night, sad and depressed. I was heartbroken thinking that my dream would never happen. The meeting had gone so well, everyone in the room had received a life-changing message. I knew spirit was helping me, so how could heaven let me down? I fell asleep and received a dream from my grandmother that changed everything.

I remember the dream like it was yesterday. It was so real that I could feel the coldness of the room and could even smell my grandmother's Jean Naté perfume. In the dream, I was walking into my grandmother's house and there was Grandma Mary sitting on the couch, waiting for me. She asked me to come sit next to her. I remember looking at her in the dream and saying, "OMG, does Mom know you're here!?" She said, *No, I am here for you.*

I was so overjoyed to see my grandmother alive and in the living room that all I could think about was running to get my mom so she could experience my grandmother there as well. Of course, my grandmother didn't let me. She was adamant that she needed to talk with me and would not allow me to leave.

She told me not to sell out. She said my path was chosen by heaven and that she was proud of me for doing this work and for delivering the messages that she was never able to. She reminded me that she had been the one leading me all along, and to have faith and listen.

She told me that one day I would have my own show and that the whole family would be involved, but at the moment it just wasn't time. She told me to stay on my path and keep doing my healing work. In the end she promised me it would happen. She told me that my path was already chosen and that I was meant to go international with my gift—reaching people on my own television show around the world and removing the fear of death.

I told her how disappointed I was, and that it was so hard to be patient, but that I would trust her words and listen to what she was telling me.

In the dream I was having a hard time understanding that it wasn't reality. I was so happy to see my grandma that I wanted everyone to know. I remember asking her to take a "selfie" in the dream, to show my mom that she was alive and well.

I remember taking out my iPhone to take a photo with her on the couch. I took out my phone and took the picture of me hugging my grandmother. When I went to look at it on the screen it was only me with my arms out. My grandmother wasn't there.

I turned to her and she laughed. I remember her kissing me, and then the next thing you know I was waking up to the sunlight shining through my bedroom window. The dream was over.

I ran to my phone and immediately checked the photos. The dream was so real I was really expecting there to be a selfie with

Grandma saved in my camera roll. Of course, the photo was not there; however, I knew she had come to me for a reason, and I had heard the message loud and clear.

After that I received more and more calls from producers. They wanted me to star in shows that were just not me. The ideas were ridiculous and ranged from "pop-up psychic" to "who's haunting my house." Those shows were not where my heart was. I wanted to be on TV helping the normal, everyday person reconnect with someone in heaven. Not playing Ghostbusters.

One of the TV concepts was so insane I actually thought it was a joke. A producer called me and wanted to produce a show about a psychic matchmaker. It sounded like something exciting until I heard the details. The producer wanted me to read a bachelor or bachelorette and ask their departed loved one whom they would marry. It wasn't something I specialized in, but I had done readings where souls in spirit predicted marriage among the living. It hadn't seemed unusual, since spirit can see tomorrow so much more clearly than we can see yesterday.

The crazy part of this show concept was that after the reading, the producers would hire a detective to find the "soul mate" that the spirit identified, and try to force them to marry the person. I was horrified by this bizarre idea and immediately knew it wouldn't work. Spirit would never force you to do something. Life is a choice and we all have free will. Yes, spirit will guide you and lead you to successful opportunities, but it will never make decisions for you or force you to marry someone. Finding your soul mate is a life choice that we need to make on our own. Needless to say, I gave that producer a hard no.

I decided to put my television dreams on hold. I listened to my grandmother's words and decided to stay on my path. For years

I stopped taking calls from producers and instead had my team screen all the calls that involved reality TV. Besides, new doors were opening up as I was asked to frequent TV morning shows and radio shows. I was adding new cities to my tour schedule and was content following the path heaven was leading me on. It allowed me to be up close and personal with fans and followers, and I enjoyed meeting so many beautiful people and souls during my tour.

One day almost five years later, I was out shopping with Alexa when my team sent me a cold call. It was a producer from MGM. Even though they had been screening the calls, once in a while they would pass someone noteworthy along. I rarely called anyone back, because I had my grandmother's words in the back of my mind reminding me to stay on my path and not sell out.

This time I looked at the message on my phone and I heard a voice inside me say, *Pick up the phone and call her back.* At the time I didn't second-guess myself—spirit spoke to me and I just did it. Alexa looked at me, a little annoyed. We were vacationing in Palm Beach and I had promised I would not make any business calls.

The woman answered and I explained that I was returning her call. She told me MGM was developing a reality TV show with a panel of psychic mediums that would be a docudrama. I thanked her for her time and told her that I was not interested. She started rambling on about what an amazing idea it was and that I was turning down the opportunity of a lifetime. I thanked her again and hung up the phone. I explained to Alexa it was just another producer trying to pitch a ridiculous show idea.

The next thing you know I heard a voice calling out "Are you kidding me!? Did you just hang up on me? Pick up the phone! Pick up the phone." No, it was not spirit, it was the producer from

MGM. Apparently, the call had never disconnected, and I could hear her voice screaming at me through my pocket.

I picked up the phone, puzzled and confused. I knew I had pressed the end call button, so how was this lady still on the phone?

I said hello in a weird and confused voice. Meanwhile Alexa was at my side telling me to hang up. She wanted to spend time together and this call was clearly getting in the way. The producer asked why I was not interested. I explained to her that this wasn't a show; it was my life. If I was going to pursue anything, it would be a show that was true to my life and that was completely focused on my work of helping and healing. She asked if she could call me back the following day and begged me to pick up. I agreed.

That night the phone rang again. She called to tell me that MGM loved me and that they were going to drop the original idea and work closely with me to develop a series centered around my life, work, and family. I was in complete awe. I could not believe it. It was just like my grandmother had said. She had told me in the dream that I would have my own show one day. Now was the time, and my dream was about to unfold.

Contracts were sent over and the next year was spent with producers flying us back and forth to LA , taking trips to my house, and getting to know every little detail about my life and my family. I could not believe this was happening.

Weeks turned into months. Little by little crews began filming and then would head back to LA. Producers came to see my shows in the evening, and then spend the day hanging out with Alexa and me to see what our day-to-day life was like.

One day I couldn't take it anymore. I wanted to know what was happening. I knew a show was being developed, but I was afraid it would fall through. I sent an email to the production team and immediately received an email back saying we needed to talk. My heart dropped into my stomach. In my experience, those words were never good. I grabbed the phone and immediately called the team. I was sweating and nervous. I had invested a year on this and could not handle bad news.

The VP answered and said, "You just got your own show on E! television network." I didn't have words; all I could do was cry. He explained that E! wanted to meet Alexa, my family, and me as early as next week. I jumped in the car and drove as fast as I could to see Alexa. She was at a dress show helping for pageant season. I walked in crying, and she immediately thought someone had died since I never cry. She said, "OMG, what's wrong? Baby, what's wrong? You're scaring me." I told her we got the show. She immediately started crying, and we were hugging in the middle of the dress show.

The customers were looking at us like we were crazy, but we didn't care. It was our dream come true. The next thing Alexa and I knew we were on a plane, headed off to the NBC Universal building with our sisters to meet with the E! executives. They told us how much they loved us and wanted to produce the show.

Not long after that, camera crews flooded my house and neighborhood. All day and night Alexa and I were being filmed for TV. I could see my grandmother standing in spirit, proud and joyful. I heard her voice saying, *I told you this day would come*—and it did!

SUGGESTED VIDEO: Google "How to watch *Meet the Frasers* on E!" to find out how you can tune in to my reality series on the E! entertainment network.

TOOLS FOR LIFE

What I learned most from my experience with television is to believe in yourself. Not everyone will share in your dream or vision, and that's okay. As long as you can see it, you can achieve it. Just because something doesn't exactly fit in your time line does not mean that heaven isn't helping you toward that goal. It just means that you need to dream big and keep believing in yourself. Ask yourself these questions, and heaven will help manifest your dream and bring it to life:

1. What do you really want in life?

2. Who can help you support this goal or dream?

3. What are the short-term goals you can work on right now to help you fulfill your dream?

Check in with yourself every day and stay on track. I believe that when you are kind, work really hard, and do things for the right reasons, heaven will help you make your dreams come true.

Remember that it is okay to say no. If an opportunity presents itself but your intuition is telling you that it's not right for you, don't be afraid to turn it down. If it is not the right time for your opportunity, it will come back to you in another way.

I believe that when it is your time, it is your time. Looking back, I am happy I didn't get the first TV opportunity. I was young and still learning about my gift. Now that I have more experience, I feel it's a much better time to share my mediumship with the world.

The same lessons can be applied in your life. When you try to make things happen before the time and opportunity is right, you may miss vital steps that you need to take. Remember that each step you take, no matter how small, is shaping your future and life. Follow your path with your whole heart and soul and do it because you love it.

When you love who you are and what you do, you will never fail.

CHAPTER 14

Ask the Medium— Questions about Life, Death, and the Afterlife

1. What is heaven?

Heaven is the beautiful and magical place our soul enters after we leave the physical world. The best way to explain heaven is that it's the ultimate paradise, a place where happiness abides, and everyone knows one another. Heaven can be compared to something that you experience in your dreams, because it can be anything you want it to be. A great dream is going to be different for everyone, and heaven is the same. You'll experience your own paradise surrounded by the things that you love.

Many times during readings loved ones will come through and show a glimpse of heaven appearing. Usually I see them in a similar setting to the places they loved and enjoyed here in this world. For example, a father who passed away might have been his happiest and most at peace when he was fishing. In heaven he will re-create this experience. A hiker who loved trekking through the woods will show up to me in a similar setting or sitting on a mountain-top. If this idea is hard to get your head around, think about it this way—heaven is energy. It is not a planet that you can land on like the moon; it is like a dream that your soul creates for all eternity. However, heaven isn't all fly fishing, golf, or whatever pastimes you enjoyed in life. In heaven you will encounter loved ones who have passed, and even relatives who died long before you were born. You will also be in the presence of angels and God.

2. What is a psychic?

A psychic is a person with a naturally heightened awareness and extrasensory perception that allow them to read the energy around a person, question, or circumstance and gain insight without any prior knowledge. Someone with psychic abilities may experience vivid visions or intense feelings that tell a story and deliver infor-mation right in front of them like a movie. Or they might feel the message as though it were happening to them, or even hear something whispered in their ear. Often psychics will experience premonitions that warn them of something that is about to happen in the future or show them a situation that is about to take place.

Everybody is born with a degree of psychic ability or intuition, but some people are more *tuned in* than others. A gifted psychic is born with a level of psychic ability that allows them to consistently perceive much more than what meets the eye.

3. What is a medium?

A medium has the unique ability to see and communicate with the departed as though they were right here with us. All mediums are psychic—they can see visions or tap into the future to some extent—but not all psychics are mediums. In my experience, mediumship is much different from what you see in the movies. Once you have accepted your gift, it is not scary or sad but rather a beautiful ability to receive messages from the other side and use it to heal and help others to overcome grief.

Mediums usually know they have the gift from a very young age when they realize they can see things that most people can't. For me, the signs started very early when I was only around three or four years old. My life was very similar to *The Sixth Sense*. My experiences first started after my grandmother passed away when I was three years old. She would come back to see me almost every night, talking to me and sitting on the edge of my bed as though she were still alive.

I believe that most young children are still connected to heaven and will see a spirit from time to time, but for me it was intensified. After my grandmother stopped visiting me, other spirits I'd never met before would come through and want me to pass messages on to their family members. It was scary for me at the time and I really wanted to avoid the whole thing, but my mother helped me thorough it. She let me know what a sacred responsibility it was to deliver healing messages from heaven to friends and neighbors.

4. How do you, a psychic medium, receive messages?

Psychic ability is almost like learning a new language. Souls on the other side relay messages that I interpret and pass on to their loved ones. The way they communicate with me is kind of unique! It's as though all of my senses open up to allow those in heaven to speak so I can interpret their message.

One way they communicate with me is visually. Often when I am reading for someone I will begin to experience quick visions and flashes, almost like a snippet of a movie in my head. It's almost like when you are reading a book. You read the words, but in your head, you *see* each scene of the book unfold as though you were right there in the story. Souls will show me important scenes from their life, and flash signs and symbols in front of me that I can interpret. Over the years I have learned to recognize and understand a vast variety of signs and symbols. If a grandmother who is in heaven flashes me a pink ribbon, then I know that the person I am reading for will be giving birth to a baby girl. If I were to see a blue ribbon, I'd know it was going to be a baby boy.

Souls on the other side also communicate audibly with names, dates, and places. I have to really listen because they talk fast and sometimes very softly. It sounds like a faint whisper of someone in my ear.

Those in spirit also communicate with me by allowing me to feel things within my body. This is the way they let me know how they passed. For instance if during a reading I begin to feel my heart race and shortness of breath, I know that the soul I am speaking to passed of a heart attack. If I begin to feel a throbbing in my head, the person in spirit is telling me they passed of something related to the brain such as trauma, aneurism, brain cancer, etcetera.

Spirit will even use the sense of smell. Sometimes I will begin to smell things that represent the person I am speaking with, such as a cigarette or cigar smoke or even a signature perfume.

When I'm doing a reading, it's a full sensory experience! All my senses come together like pieces of a puzzle that allow me to experience the life of the person I'm connecting with, and pass their messages on to the intended recipient.

5. Do pets go to heaven?

It's true that all pets go to heaven. In fact, your pets are among the first to greet you when you transition. Pets have souls, and anything that comes from God goes back to God. Why do you think that humans and animals have such a strong relationship and bond with one another? Soul recognizes soul. The soul that is inside us connects so beautifully with other living beings and creatures. It is not uncommon for the departed to come through in a reading holding the pet they loved here in this world. I've seen people come through accompanied by everything from cats and dogs to horses and chickens.

The funniest reading I can remember was at an event in Manchester, New Hampshire. I was walking down the aisle, sharing messages, when a grandmother in spirit pointed to her granddaughter, saying, *Come talk to her.* I walked over to the girl and started describing her grandmother. The girl seemed rather unmoved by the messages and just sat quietly until her grandmother showed me a bunny sitting on her lap and said, *Show her the bunny.*

I told the young girl, "You are going to think I'm crazy, but your grandmother keeps holding up this bunny, telling me to show you."

The reaction on her face was priceless as she stood up and yelled, "Oh my goodness, that's my pet bunny Samson that passed!" The girl started to cry, she was so amazed by the fact that her grandmother had found her bunny in heaven and was taking care of him. It was a beautiful reminder that even if your pets get to heaven before you, there will be someone to look after them for you.

6. Do the departed work in heaven?

The departed have jobs in heaven but they're not like the jobs we have here on earth. Heaven is the ultimate paradise, but often those on the other side will choose to help people in the physical world who are struggling. Earth is the classroom where we learn our life lessons before making our transition into heaven. Many souls will watch over and help those in this world who are faced with similar struggles that they experienced during their life.

For example, someone who passed of a drug overdose will often make it their mission to watch over those in the physical world who are going through a similar experience and help them to find their way to sobriety.

7. How can I tell if my loved one is with me?

There are so many ways that your loved ones in heaven let you know they are with you. They will often speak through signs and symbols. Some of the coincidences you experience are really your loved ones in heaven giving you a sign to let you know they're around.

Signs from heaven will come to you if you're open to receiving them. Look for them and they will start to appear. You don't have to do anything to start communicating—when spirit knows you're listening, you'll begin to see signs.

You might be driving and see your mother's name written on a license plate, or your dad's favorite bird may fly over and sit next to you as you sit outside drinking your morning coffee. Souls on the other side have amazing ways of getting your attention and letting you know they are there. Anytime you see something that brings back a memory that you and your loved one shared, or if you see something that reminds you of them, chances are it is a sign they are sending you from above.

A very dear friend of mine lost her mom after a long and hard battle with Parkinson's disease. Before her mom passed, my friend whispered in her ear, *Mom, I want you to send me pennies from heaven, so I know that you made it to the other side.*

She didn't really think much about the pennies and proceeded to the funeral home to arrange for her mom's services. When she walked back out to her car in the empty parking lot, right next to the driver's-side door were two pennies. She picked them up and wondered if it could really be her mom trying to communicate and let her know that she had made it into heaven. She continued back to her house, and when she arrived she got a phone call from her neighbor, asking her if she would like to come over for a glass of wine. Once there she took a seat at the kitchen table and her friend brought her a wineglass. But when the neighbor went to grab a coaster, a penny was laying there on top. The neighbor was a little confused, as she had just cleaned the whole house and table and had no idea how she had missed the penny. My friend knew for sure that penny was from her mom. She now keeps a jar by her bedside filled with pennies that her mom has sent to her.

8. What is intuition? Does everyone have it?

Everyone is born with some level of intuition, which is the ability to feel things on a deeper level and look for insights to help with your life. Intuition can help with everything from finding lost items to deciding on a job offer. Intuition can also keep you out of harm's way. Have you ever heard a voice in your head say, *Slow down!* or *Change lanes!* right before a car skids in front of you or gets into an accident where you were supposed to be?

What about when you are lost and cannot find your way home? When you calm down and listen, your intuition becomes your own internal GPS guiding you to the right routes and roads to take you home safely.

Even if you're not a practicing psychic, you can use your intuition to help other people make decisions. Have you ever had a friend call to tell you about a new person they just started dating? They might be ecstatic over how well everything is going and what a wonderful time they are having together. On the outside you're happy and excited for them, congratulating them and sharing their enjoyment, but in your gut, you know it will not last. Almost always, a week later you get a fateful call reporting the breakup you knew was inevitable.

The opposite holds true as well. Sometimes you know a friend has found their forever love long before they do, and you get to just sit back and nod when you hear of the upcoming nuptials.

9. Is psychic ability or mediumship inherited?

It is very common for psychic ability or mediumship to be passed down within a family. There have also been instances, under extreme circumstances, where psychic ability occurs out of nowhere or when people have near-death experiences.

I often hear stories of people who were in a coma after a car accident and, after awakening, discovered they could see and hear the departed. One time I even met a man who was struck by lightning, after which he was able to communicate with the dead and experience psychic visions. Near-death experiences can open up awareness when someone gets so close to the other side. It's an eye-opener that strengthens their connection between this world and the next.

Personally, I have never had a near-death experience. In my family my grandmother was psychic and passed the gift down to my mother, who in turn passed it down to me. I am not sure why the departed chose to talk to my family, but I believe it is because we have always been open and receptive to listening to them.

10. Are there times when you are not able to reach someone in heaven?

There have been rare occasions when I have not been able to reach a particular soul that I was trying to connect with. When this occurs, I tell my clients not to jump to any conclusions. This does not mean that the person has not made it to heaven—only that there were factors blocking the connection at that particular time or place. Deep grief can block a reading because the client may not be ready to hear a message, or the soul on the other side may not feel it will help them emotionally.

Another reason for a failure to connect might be that the person has not been gone long enough. When someone has passed away in less than a year's time, it can be very hard to reach them. They are able to watch over their loved ones, but not get a clear message to me, or any medium. I always know when someone has passed within the year because when I try to connect with them I won't hear or see anything at all—or it will sound garbled or full of static. The best way I can describe this is that it's very similar to when we change residences here in the physical world. Normally we have to get a new phone number and wait a year or so until our name, number, and address are listed in the Yellow Pages. It takes about a year to truly get settled into a new place, and it's the same with those on the other side. They usually have to build up enough energy before they can come through and pass on a message.

11. If someone passes from illness, are they still sick on the other side?

The best part about heaven is that there are no cemeteries, and everyone lives forever without illness or pain. It is amazing to see those who were so sick in life become happy, healthy, and whole in heaven, and to witness the comfort that loved ones receive when they realize their dad who could not walk before he passed away is now running around.

One of the most inspiring stories I like to share about the miracles heaven brings happened to me at a live event. I saw a young boy standing behind a woman. I walked over to tell her a young boy was standing behind her and asked if this was her son. She nodded and started to cry as I received visions of the traumatic illness her son had faced here in this world. He showed me images of himself in a wheelchair and having to be fed by a feeding tube, unable to speak. Then he showed me that he had been cured immediately upon entering heaven. He wanted his mom to let go of the feeling that she didn't do enough for him. He remembered the times she had brought over other children to play with him, quit her day job to take care of him, and devoted her life to making sure his needs were met and that he had lived a normal life. He remembered sharing a last birthday before he transitioned into heaven and wanted his mom to know that he was fine now, just like all the other kids. He kept telling her, *If only you could see me now! You would not worry. You'd see that I have no more pain. I am free!*

Pain, suffering, and illness are all things that living beings on earth are faced with. Once we transition to the other side, all that is left behind, and we can begin our new life in paradise.

12. What messages do the departed have for us while we're in the physical world?

Enjoy the journey! When you are born here on earth you are given a life's mission or destiny to fulfill. You have special gifts that are yours alone, to be used to help change the world. Everyone's gift or talent is unique and beautiful in its own way. The souls on the other side want you to appreciate and embrace your gifts. Whether you have been blessed with the gift of singing, writing, communication, teaching, leadership, or whatever—make the most of it! People tend to hit roadblocks when they stray away from their natural talents, but the minute they take steps to embrace them, doors open, and new opportunities emerge.

13. When I dream of loved ones in heaven, is it really them?

Yes, many times loved ones will visit in your dreams to validate their presence and allow you to know they have not gone far. It is easier for loved ones to appear in dreams than during your daily activities. After all, they are energy and can easily slip into a dream and connect with your subconscious. When you are sleeping, your mind is still and dormant, with none of the normal distractions. That makes it very easy for them to get your attention and reach you without having to push past the thousands of thoughts that are buzzing around in your mind throughout the day.

During the day life can get so busy that you might miss out on seeing the signs and symbols that those in heaven send you. Your loved ones can only reach you when you allow yourself to relax and allow your brain to cool down, and the perfect time for this is in your sleep.

Those in heaven will only come to you in a dream if doing so will help you and allow you to move past your grief. They will not come through if you cannot handle it or if they feel that seeing them might be overwhelming for you. Some of my clients don't experience dreams of their loved ones because their grief is too fresh. When someone passes on it is a new beginning, both for the soul who has passed, and the people left behind. Souls in heaven do not want you to hang on to them too tightly or to get obsessed with searching for messages. They want you to continue moving forward in your own life and pursue your dreams. This doesn't mean that they don't love you. They care about you so much that they do not want you to cry or grieve over their passing. Later on, as you move past the grief phase, they will come back to you in dreams, but only once in a while. Often the departed will appear in family members' dreams when a major event is taking place in their life to let them know they are sharing this milestone!

14. Can psychic mediums read your mind?

Psychic mediums can do many amazing things, but reading minds is actually not one of them. You will witness them receiving messages from the departed, and it might feel like they are reading your thoughts as well. In fact, they are not reading your mind, but rather listening to the spirit world and feeling out the energy to see the different opportunities that are around you. Sometimes it can seem like psychic mediums can read your mind because the other side will tell them what you are doing, or share your future goals and plans. For example, if you are thinking about selling your house and moving to California, the other side will probably tell me this and maybe share the time frame of it happening or even recommend things that you can do to help smooth over the transition.

Many times people will walk into a reading thinking, *I hope that he tells me about my husband's health*, or, *I hope he tells me if I am going to get that job I just applied for*, and usually those things will come up during the reading. Even though it seems like a big coincidence, it happens because those on the other side tune in to your thoughts so that they can give you guidance. This is why I recommend thinking about what questions you have for spirit before a reading. I've found that they will answer your questions without you even having to bring it up to the medium!

Being a psychic is very similar to being a translator—we just take what the spirit world tells us, and put it together so that you can understand.

15. What about family who passed before I was born—are they around me too?

So many times my clients become confused when a family member who passed away before my client was born pops into a reading. Family is family, and even if they passed one thousand years ago, you can rest assured that they are with you in spirit despite the fact you never met in life. Souls in heaven don't pick and choose who they will watch over and who they won't. If there is a connection, they will be there. And you have probably already met—often we meet these same family members on the other side before we are born into this world. Family members in heaven will stand by you during birth and help your soul make the transition to the physical world.

Although you may not have met them here in the physical world, you will be reunited with them after you make your transition into heaven.

16. What is my loved ones' advice for dealing with their passing?

Your loved ones want you to be encouraged by their passing and be at peace knowing that they are well and in the presence of God. As

I've said, they want you to live life to the fullest, and not let their passing get in the way of that.

17. What language do they speak in heaven?

In heaven everyone is able to speak a universal language. The best part about heaven is that communication is so seamless. From what I am told, souls on the other side communicate telepathically and everyone is able to understand one another. I'm told that even pets are able to communicate with us once we reach the other side.

18. Are my loved ones in heaven angry or upset with me?

Transitioning to heaven with anger and resentment is like bringing your barbells on a canoe trip. They are too heavy and it just won't work. Heavy emotions must be *checked at the door* to allow the soul to enter heaven. If any trace of misunderstanding or hurt remains, the life review takes care of that. The emotions that souls are left with are pure love, joy, and compassion.

19. What should I do with the belongings my loved ones have left behind?

All mediums connect differently and I don't need a physical object to make a connection, but back in the day, psychics used to hold an article that belonged to the deceased to help the spirits come through. I've had people bring the weirdest things to my shows. A woman recently came to an event with her husband's eyeballs in a plastic bag filled with saline. Your loved ones are happy that you have something to remember them by, but don't feel obligated to keep their organs or everything they ever owned.

I had a woman come to my show whose grandfather had just passed. The whole family came, hoping he would come through. The granddaughter was devastated because she hadn't been able to say good-bye to him. He came through, and he wanted her to have his shirt. She kept saying that she didn't know how she could get his shirt; everything had been given to charity. He kept insisting that his shirt was in the car. Suddenly her aunt jumped up! "I have his shirt—I picked up his belongings from the hospital and they're still in my trunk." The grandfather knew that, and wanted his granddaughter to have something of his—not because his soul was contained in it but as a sweet reminder that he was with her.

That said, don't feel you have to hang on to something if you can't afford to keep it. Spirit will have access to the memories of that item in heaven and that's what matters. When you die, you create your own heaven out of your memories, so you might find yourself driving your beloved '62 Mustang long after it's been reduced to scrap metal here on earth!

20. How are you able to read people over the phone? Don't you have to be in person?

I don't have to be sitting with you to give an accurate reading. In fact, I do my best work when I'm on the phone. It's easy to get distracted by visual cues and facial expressions in person or on Skype—but when I'm on the phone I can tune in to spirit and my client's energy, and that is what works best for me.

21. When you conduct a reading, are you bothering or disturbing my loved in heaven?

Not at all! It is important to remember that those on the other side are energy and can be in multiple places at once. As a medium I do not bring your loved ones to you during a reading, you bring them to me. They are around you and watching over you as you make your way in life. A reading is like having a direct connection to heaven, much like talking on a telephone. It does not disturb or bother the soul at all. Often those in heaven are so excited to connect with their living family members that they show up early in anticipation and start talking before I even meet with my client!

22. Why are some spirits quieter than others?

Everyone's different, including souls in heaven. How much they share depends on their personality and the messages they have. If a mother in spirit was a big gossiper and talkative when she was here in this world, you better believe her larger-than-life personality will come through in spirit the same way it did in the physical world. Someone who was reserved and quiet in life may take a step backward and let another spirit take the spotlight and pass on the message. Sometimes the message itself determines why some souls come through louder or stronger than others. If spirit has an urgent message to share, they will push forward to pass on the information.

I have noticed that souls have a lot of urgency to come through when there are unanswered questions around the person's passing or death. At a recent live event, a soul came through loud and clear, flagging me down from across the room, and telling me that she had to speak with her daughter. I walked over to the daughter, held her hand, and began to see flashes of her mom's unexpected passing and the underlying circumstances. Her mom had passed unexpectedly in an airplane while sitting next to her daughter on the way back from vacation. Her daughter had begged the mom to go on the trip with her and was now feeling terrible guilt, thinking it was her fault that her mom had passed away. Her mom had been through an autopsy and there was no explanation for why she experienced heart complications during the flight. The mother came through loud and clear with a life-changing message. She wanted her daughter to know that it was not her fault; her death was caused by a blood clot that had traveled to her heart, which had nothing to do with her vacation. In fact, she explained that God had given them a little extra mother-daughter time before the mother made her transition into heaven. She wanted her daughter to know that she loved the vacation they had shared together and wanted her daughter to look back on the photos and remember the beautiful way her mom had left this world while she was loving and enjoying life.

23. Do angels exist?

Absolutely! Angels do exist. They are known for their loving nature and their comforting presence. Angels walk beside us every day, protecting and guiding us. Have you ever felt sad and lonely, or been crying over a situation—then felt a sense of comfort. That comfort came from your angels as they surrounded you with their presence and love.

We all have guardian angels around us, sending signals through our intuition to let us know they are there when we need them. You can talk with your angels any time you feel afraid or sad, and you'll immediately feel their warm, loving energy put you at ease. Angels are like the search-and-rescue team of heaven. They are always there when tragedy strikes. Often when there is a tragedy or mass casualty, angels rush in to carry the souls of those who are affected directly to the other side so that they will not feel any pain or suffering.

You know your angels are there when you hear that little voice in your head that tells you to stay away from something or to use caution while driving.

24. Do children have the ability so see and hear the departed?

It's common for family members who have departed to come back and visit children. It's amazing how many stories I hear of children who accurately describe grandparents and family members who passed away years before they were born. Do not worry if a child you know has this experience; it simply means that they are protected and have been visited by spirit. These experiences are real and provide a beautiful reminder that our loved ones are always there, watching and looking after us.

Since children are very young and innocent, they don't question these visits. Many times children do not even know that they are seeing or experiencing a soul who has passed because to them, it's simply a lovely presence that comes to play with them. I believe this is why so many children talk about imaginary friends—in fact, these friends are spirit guides, deceased loved ones, and angels.

25. How do those in heaven want to be remembered?

Our loved ones in heaven want us to remember them in a way that comforts us and brings a smile to our face. Their message for the living is that they want us to remember them happy, healthy, and full of life. Often a loved one will come through to me appearing as they did before they became sick, old, or weak. It's always so inspiring to see those who passed away from illness come through looking their best and all put back together. They do not want us to remember them as they were when they were sick, or to think about how they left this world. They'd like us to remember them in their prime, when they were able to spend happy times with us and enjoy the gift of life. Sometimes during readings, spirits will reach out to their loved ones and say, *I am so sorry that you had to see me like that, but rest assured, I am fine now.* A man who had his legs amputated because of diabetes will come through on the other side dancing, running, and showing his family that he has legs again and can move freely. A grandfather who was always losing his dentures may come through and smile—showing his family that he has his teeth again. A mother who passed away from cancer will come through flipping her hair, showing her family that it has grown back after radiation and chemotherapy in this world.

Our loved ones do not want us to feel sad or hold on to the pain of watching their bodies change while they transitioned from earth to heaven. They want to let you know that they are completely at peace and whole again.

26. How often should you get a reading?

A reading from a medium is an amazing tool that can provide valuable insight, clarity, and healing from grief. Those on the other side love to help in any way they can, whether through a psychic reading or by reaching out with a sign or a symbol. Although a psychic reading is a good way to receive insights, tools, and techniques to help you improve your life, I recommend you limit readings to once every year or so. A psychic reading will give you about a year's worth of information, but remember, you are meant to live your own life, not be guided 24/7 by the spirits.

It is not possible to always make the right decisions. We were designed to learn through trial and error. It's perfectly normal to have questions and to occasionally make the wrong choice. Earth is a classroom where we learn so many valuable life lessons, and where each one of us discovers our life's mission. Your loved ones on the other side can give you insight, but they cannot make decisions for you.

I often get asked about relationships during readings. *Should I be in a relationship with Joe or Michael?* The other side can describe that person to you in detail. They can share their specific characteristics such as personality, way of life, and energy. But they won't tell you who to choose because they would be living your life for you.

A psychic reading is kind of like driving a car from the East Coast. In a reading you may be told your destination is California and you may be given some tips on how to get there, but it is your responsibility to navigate and get yourself to that destination. Spirit can only advise and lend a helping hand to keep you on track. You have to let life unfold and enjoy the journey and the beautiful life lessons along the way.

27. Do you ever see death in a reading?

Thankfully, no. I can't remember a time when I was told that some-one would pass during a reading. The first reason for this is that nobody knows when you are going to pass, other than God himself, not even a psychic or a medium. Second, during a reading those on the other side will only bring forward information that is for your highest and best good and that will allow you to live your life to the fullest. They don't want you to focus on the day you're going to pass and live your life in fear.

Don't get me wrong, there are times when souls on the other side will caution or warn you of impending danger, but they're not trying to scare you. Anything that's told to you during a reading can be changed, because of the power of free will. Spirit is not there to tell you that you are going to get sick or you are going to break your leg on vacation. Instead they will give you information to help keep it from happening, like *wear a helmet* or *get a flu shot.*

One day a client called with questions about her love life. She was surprised when I began talking about her stomach pains that the other side said were caused by her ovaries. They kept speaking of three round disks. I urged her to go to the doctor to get it checked out and she did. She called me a few weeks later to say that the doctor had found three round cysts on her ovaries. She was worried because she did not have children and didn't want to lose the ability to have them in the future. However, because of the reading she was able to get them taken care of early and avoided a major problem.

This is the perfect example of how spirit reaches out to help us. They do not want us to be scared or frightened by them or by death itself, but if they can help us or protect us along the way, they will.

28. Do you ever use your psychic ability for gambling or the lottery?

I love a good casino, but if I were you, I wouldn't follow me around the slot machines because my gift doesn't work that way. Occasionally my intuition leads me to a machine, and I feel from the energy around it that it's ready to pay off, but that's no different from the hunches that we all get sometimes. Sometimes people feel like they should buy a lottery ticket or enter a contest—and it works. Alexa had a feeling she would win the Miss Rhode Island pageant, so she entered, and she won! But it took a ton of hard work to make her hunch a reality. You can't use your ability to cheat life. By all means let your intuition guide you, but you also have to work toward a goal, enjoy the journey, and always come from a place of love and compassion. It's as simple as this: If you work hard and are kind, amazing things will come to you.

29. Are those on the other side ever wrong?

Those in heaven are never wrong, but remember, their message is coming through a mortal—the medium. I might be talking to a soul and see him playing checkers when he really played backgammon. Spirit sends the right signal, but sometimes I misinterpret it. The messages can be confusing or families can be complicated with divorces and adoptions. It's easy for the medium or the recipient to mix people up. Spirit is never biased. Even if someone was controlling in life, they leave their own agenda behind when they die and will only give you advice that's in your own best interest. But when you're translating the language of spirit, there's always room for interpretation. Usually between the medium and the person receiving the message, we can figure it out!

30. How would you describe a reading with you?

The first thing I do before each reading is say a prayer that the message for the client will come through loud and clear and help with any problems they are facing. I don't use tarot cards, crystals, tea leaves, or other tools. As soon as I sit down with my client or speak with them over the phone, I start getting quick flashes of information that helps me provide insight to that person. Family members who have passed on will step forward and make their presence known. They'll come through with memories of time spent together, communicating in a way that lets their personality shine through. If you had an uncle who had a funny personality in life, he may come through and tease you or joke with you like he did when he was alive. I always ask spirit for specific information and not generalities, so the person who is getting the reading will know and recognize that it is really their loved one. The souls I connect with come through with validations in many different ways. They tell me the names of the people who are with them in heaven, important dates such as birthdays, anniversaries, and family gatherings, and they show me what they look like. It's almost like having a family reunion with those you lost in heaven!

During a reading I never ask questions about what the person who is getting the reading is coming to me for. There is no need because those on the other side already know what is going on in your life. After introductions are made and I inform the person I am reading about their loved ones who are with them in spirit, I ask the soul in heaven to relay any messages they have. It's amazing to see the transformational healing power those messages provide.

A husband whose wife feels guilty for taking him off life support will come through and talk about how he's at peace, assuring his wife that she did the right thing. Children who passed at a young age will come through to reassure their parents that they are safe and will often let their parents know that a grandmother or other loved one is with them in heaven. If someone passed away peacefully, they may simply come through to share favorite memories, moments, and celebrations they enjoyed here in the physical world.

It's important to remember that those in heaven are completely fine. They don't want you to worry about them but to enjoy, celebrate, and embrace the life that you are living.

31. Is there ever any negative information that comes through in a reading?

Information given through a reading is intended to help us improve our lives. Some information that spirit shares may be surprising and not what you expected, and it may feel negative. People going through a painful breakup might be upset when they are told to keep their options open because the person they are so upset about is just not the one for them. Despite their reaction, this message is intended to be a gentle nudge from the soul's divine perspective, so that their loved one on earth will move on and find the right person. You always have the power of free will, and anything that comes through in a reading can change depending on your actions.

A client of mine had been dating a man who was recently divorced. She would see him on and off, but he was distant and it was heartbreaking to her. She wanted to be married and have a family with him. He would promise her the world, but they were only promises. She was reluctant to break ties with him and came to me hoping that spirit would see the two of them happily married and living together. However, spirit didn't see this man in her future and told her to keep her options open. They saw a man coming into her life and said his name was Kevin. They showed me that Kevin would pursue her and want to marry her. She wasn't as open to this information as I expected, since her heart was set on her current boyfriend, but she wrote it all down and left. About six months later a man named Kevin came into her life. They were married about a year after meeting and are planning on having children. This was the happy ending that her reading had forecast! Another time a wife called me up, worried about her relationship with her husband. They had been argu-ing constantly and she was afraid their bickering would lead to divorce. Her father on the other side stepped in and clearly saw what was going on. He showed me that the couple lived in the same house but lived two separate lives. They did not speak to each other, had separate friends, and were on completely different schedules. Thanks to her deceased father, I was able to offer the woman ways to bring her relationship back to life. Her father's advice was simple—*start from scratch and enjoy the simple things with each other. Take walks together, sit down and share a meal, spend time just talking, and bring the love and romance back into the rela-tionship.* The woman began to cry; the message hit home for her. She said that she and her husband had drifted so far apart because of their busy lives. She took her father's advice and their relationship became stronger than ever.

Those on the other side can see tomorrow so much more clearly than we see today, and will only tell us something that appears negative if they can provide a positive solution.

32. As a psychic medium, can you read yourself?

Yes, I can read myself occasionally, but I don't get the kind of detailed reading I would give to someone else. Honestly, I believe my gift is not intended to be used on myself but to encourage others to open their eyes to what lies on the other side, and to use that knowledge to heal. Don't get me wrong, from time to time I receive insights and premonitions about my own life, but I don't have the ability to cheat life or predict the winning Powerball numbers. The way that I receive my own personal messages is very similar to the way that I teach others to tune in and receive messages for themselves. I will be shown signs or symbols letting me know that I am on the right path. And, of course, my loved ones in heaven visit me from time to time.

I remember one of the first readings that came through for me happened just as I was getting in tune with my psychic gift, after pushing it away for many years. My grandmother came to me in a vision and told me that I would touch many lives as a psychic medium. She explained that it was a calling I was meant to pursue. At the time, I had no idea what she was talking about—I was in school, learning to become an EMT and planning on furthering my education to become a paramedic. Maybe, after I had completed my schooling, I would read for friends and family on the side.

I guess I was wrong and my grandmother was right because word of mouth began to spread like wildfire. As people heard about the boy who could *speak to the dead* I started getting calls from all over Rhode Island and across the East Coast who were seeking my help. Soon I was invited to be on small radio shows and to appear on local TV news stations—and before I knew it my journey as a professional psychic medium had begun.

33. How do you choose which spirits come through at a live event?

During any event or group reading I like to pretend that I run the show, but really, it's those on the other side who do. I am like an usher at a theater, letting those on the other side step forward one by one to allow me to share their messages. There are a lot of factors that determine which spirits come through during a session. One of the first factors is the urgency of the message. I've had spirits race to the front of the line during a live event to pass on a message they had not been able to communicate in life. A young child who died suddenly is determined to let his parents know that he or she is okay, and that the accident wasn't their fault. A father who had a difficult relationship with his daughter wants her to know he was struggling with an alcohol addiction.

Another factor that comes into play is personality. Spirits who had an outgoing personality in life will be the first to jump up and try to get a message to their family. Spirits who were more reserved in life tend to be pushed toward the back of the line.

Those in spirit will come through with a message for the people who need to hear it the most. It is amazing to see the comfort, love, and reassurance given by spirit through each reading. Although not everyone receives a direct reading during a live event, those on the other side do an amazing job of getting indirect messages to their loved ones so that they know that they are safe and at peace.

34. Does it matter if you are cremated or buried?

There are times when I do a reading and it comes up that the departed had wished to be buried, but was cremated instead.

A woman came to an event and was worried because her family cremated her father because they couldn't afford a burial. He had made it clear when he was alive that he didn't want to be cremated. She was so upset that she was actually having bad dreams that her father came back and was angry with her. But the dreams were not from her father—they were from her own guilt. Her dad came through and said he hadn't believed in the afterlife. He had wanted his body whole. He knew differently now, and he told his daughter that what happened to his earthly body didn't matter at all. She should release the guilt and go on with her life.

35. Are those in heaven with me when I am visiting their grave?

Once I was channeling a woman whose mother had died. The mother showed me her grave lined with beer cans. I told the woman what I was seeing and she couldn't believe it. She told me that every Sunday she took her lawn chair and played music, sat back in her chair and drank beer. *Stay away from my grave!* The mother said. *Stop wasting your time there—I'm with you every day.* The mother saw that the daughter was getting married, and she let the daughter know that she had seen her dress. There's nothing wrong with visiting a loved one's grave; it can be comforting to have a special place to honor them. But know they're with you wherever you are.

36. Can those in heaven watch over many people at once?

Absolutely! Spirit is not limited by the normal restrictions; it's like a rainbow that everyone can see.

37. Do divorced people sometimes get back together in heaven?

I did a reading for a woman and her parents came through. She was furious when I told her that and called me a fraud! "My parents HATED each other! They would never be together now. We hated my father because he walked out on us." Her father had been an alcoholic, and his drinking had alienated him from his family. He wasn't able to love them, or himself, because of the drinking. She said, "My father couldn't be in heaven! He doesn't deserve to be there." She missed the point. Heaven is where we have the opportunity to release ourselves from resentment, anger, and addictions. Her parents came through with the intention of showing their daughter this, but she wasn't ready to accept and receive their message. What a shame!

On the other hand, a couple who had been married for many years got sick of each other. They separated for a while and even divorced officially, but they wound up getting back together before they died. They were together in heaven and their son was so relieved. He had been worried that because they weren't officially married when they died, they wouldn't be together. But true soul mates are always together in heaven, no paperwork or marriage license required.

SUGGESTED VIDEO: Interested in learning more? Visit MeetMattFraser.com/blog/. Each month I post new articles to help you stay connected with those you love in heaven and also to help you tap into your own psychic abilities.

T O O L S   F O R   L I F E

There are certain times when you miss your loved ones in heaven even more than usual. Special occasions like weddings, birthdays, graduations, and holidays can be bittersweet when someone special is no longer there to share the joy. But you don't have to be a medium to feel the presence of your departed loved ones. Your thoughts and words are more powerful than you realize! If you'd like to feel the presence of a friend or family member in heaven on a special day, or anytime, here are some ways to do it—no medium required!

- Invite loved ones in heaven to be part of your special day. Celebrating significant events with Mom or Grandpa doesn't have to end at their funeral. They are still there, protecting you and cheering you on, so include them in the festivities! You might put a photo of them on the mantel among the holiday decorations, or cook a special dish that they loved. You can even start a tradition of going around the table during the holiday meal and sharing special memories with your loved ones.

- Before you gather with family for a special event, take time for a quiet ritual to reach out to a loved one in the spirit world. Sit quietly and focus on your breath, or take a meditative walk around the block. A few minutes of silence in which you allow your to-do list to fade will allow you to feel the comforting presence of your loved one, which will stay with you throughout your day. Taking a few minutes to make that connection will get your event off to a "heavenly" start.

- Ask questions. As you go about your day, feel free to call on spirit to guide you. Wondering if the turkey is ready to come out of the oven? Mom has a great vantage point from heaven! Ask her for help silently or out loud. Need to know if your sister's new boyfriend is a keeper? Send a message to Dad with your thoughts, and wait for him to send you a "yay or nay" sign. He'll find a way to get you just the insight you need.

- Have fun! Souls in heaven are drawn to love and laughter, so don't feel guilty about having a good time without them. Smile and enjoy yourself, and they'll draw near to add to the love!

• ACKNOWLEDGMENTS •

No word a lie, this book was like having a baby! Nine long months of putting chapters together, getting feedback, rewriting and rephrasing. There were many sleepless nights and long days but now we have beautiful baby! Well, sort of . . .

Luckily, I had an amazing team to help me through the process. Their excitement has helped me to make this book the best that it could possibly be.

Alexa, thank you for sharing this dream with me. You are always pushing me to be the best I can be. I love having you by my side. I owe you great big hot fudge sundae.

Thank you to my mom, Angela, and my sister, Maria, for traveling to New York with me to make this book deal happen.

To my publicist, Imal Wagner, you have been with me from literally day one! Can you believe we are still here working together almost ten years later? Thank you for working so many long nights and hours to make this dream a reality. Thank you for introducing me to Simon & Schuster and for this amazing opportunity. You are a bad ass.

Thank you to my executive producer, Lisa Tucker, for incorporating my booking into *Meet the Frasers*. It is because of you that my fans and followers were able to be with me through this process and see behind the scenes.

To my editor, Jeremie Ruby-Strauss, you were the first person I met at Simon & Schuster and one I will never forget. Thank you for believing in the vision of my book and for putting it into production. Just remember, man Spanx for life!

And to Jeremie's right hand, Brita Lundberg, thank you for your tireless hard work and patience in keeping us organized, coordinated, and on schedule. You have been a life saver!

John Vairo, OMG you made it happen! Thank you for bringing my vision to life and making my book look like a bestseller. The cover is gorgeous! I love the energy it gives off. Thank you for having a great eye!

Jen Bergstrom, thank you for allowing me to put this book into the hands of millions! I will be thinking of you when I walk into the bookstore and see it proudly displayed on the shelf.

Aimee Bell, thank you for answering the one email that started this all.

Jen Robinson, thank you for taking so many meetings with me and pushing the book along to meet with the timing of my TV show. It was a close call, but we did it! I cannot wait for the press tour and book signings to begin.

Thank you to Jaime Putorti for making my book look like an actual book. I think the fans are going to LOVE it!

Thank you to Caroline Pallotta, Allison Green, and Iris Chen for always making sure that everything ran on time.

Thank you to Sarah Wright for cleaning up the grammar, spelling, and punctuation. I could have used someone like you in high school!

Thank you to Mike Kwan for actually getting this book to the printer! I can only imagine what happens behind the scenes.

To the entire team at Simon & Schuster, this has been my dream and I am forever thankful to you all. Who would have thought that someone who nearly failed English is now a published author! It just goes to show that if you can dream it, you can do it.

To Alice and Patrick Charlier, my marketing directors: Thank you for bringing my brand to the next level. You two always have the answer. You are the perfect power couple!

To Ricardo Couto, my director of security and transportation: thank you for always going the extra mile. Thank you for driving my family and me to the many NYC meetings and giving up so much of your time to make that happen.

To Sherry Ferdinandi, my CFO. Thank you for putting the little numbers in the tiny boxes. You have helped me to build an incredible team of professionals.

Thank you to NBC Universal, E! Entertainment, and MGM's Evolution Media for giving me this amazing television opportunity. I am so grateful to share my family with the world.

Thank you to Diane Miller of Diane Miller Photography in Cranston, Rhode Island, for the many family pictures and all of your support for the book and for the TV series. You have been such a team player and I value all of your hard work.

Thank you to Ashlee Hall, associate producer of *Meet the Frasers* and provider of the behind-the-scenes photos. Thank you for the coffee runs, car rides, and all your help with the series.

To Richard Bowler, my associate executive producer: thank you for being so proud of Alexa and me, and for keeping in contact with us after all of these months of filming. I am happy to now call you a friend.

Thank you to Brian Dee, director of photography for *Meet*

the Frasers, and provider of the-behind-the-scenes photos. We so enjoyed our time with you on set! Thank you for all the amazing shots and for making this series look the best it can be!

Thank you to Carine Bogossian and Adriel Bencosme, my lead creatives. Thank you for being with me from the beginning! I remember you helping me to build my first website. Because of you I now have awesome content to share with my fans worldwide.

Thank you to Rachel Rodgers Photography, for the event photos.

Thank you to Tam Dinh, my former boss at Seaport World Trade Center, for the courtesy photo.

Thank you to Judy Garrow, our childhood photographer, for the courtesy photo and for being there to capture the moment.

Even though I speak to people who have died, you don't have to be dead to find me. The best part about my job is being able to connect with people like you! I hope you will keep in touch with me by joining me on my social media channels. I love posting daily inspiration and ways for you to connect with your own loved ones in spirit. All of the accounts below are really me! You will find me doing Facebook Live broadcasts, posting pictures and videos from my tour, and sharing pictures of Alexa and me with our cats. I hope that my posts not only inspire you but also welcome you into my personal life behind the scenes.

So what are you waiting for?! Take out your phone and leave me a comment or a like. I would love to hear from you and I hope to meet you when I am in your area. Who knows, I may even be able to share a message for you from someone in spirit!

Facebook.com/MeetMattFraser

Pinterest.com/MeetMattFraser

@MeetMattFraser

@MeetMattFraser

@MeetMattFraser

Love Learning about the Afterlife?

Join my Emails from Heaven newsletter to receive videos, articles, and monthly inspirational emails to help you discover your own psychic gifts and connect with your loved ones in spirit.

Visit MeetMattFraser.com and then click on newsletter signup toward the bottom of the home page.